the 5 secrets of marriage
from the HEART

JACK ROSENBLUM & CORINNE DUGAS

TATE PUBLISHING, LLC

"The Five Secrets of Marriage from the Heart"

by Jack Rosenblum and Corinne Dugas

Copyright © 2006 by RSI, Inc. All rights reserved.

Published in the United States of America

by Tate Publishing, LLC

127 East Trade Center Terrace

Mustang, OK 73064

(888) 361–9473

Book design copyright © 2006 by Tate Publishing, LLC. All rights reserved.

This book is designed to provide accurate and authoritative information with regard to the subject matter covered. This information is given with the understanding that neither the author nor Tate Publishing, LLC is engaged in rendering legal, professional advice. Since the details of your situation are fact dependent, you should additionally seek the services of a competent professional.

ISBN: 1-5988638-8-6

DEDICATION

We dedicate this book to the memory of
our respective parents:

Harvey and Dorothy Rosenblum (married 60 years)
and
Connie and C.V. (Bud) Dugas (married 50 years)

They were wonderful role models, showing us
what it means to be committed, loving marriage
partners. And they also gave us each other.

We also dedicate this book to our daughter Currie, the
other love of our lives, in the hope that it might be part
of her educational legacy from us.

ACKNOWLEDGEMENTS

We are blessed in having a number of friends who were willing to read early drafts and give us their candid comments and critiques. We want to thank and acknowledge the following for their skillful and loving help: *Susanna Bensinger, Larry Brown, Neil Cohen, Kathy Dunn, Emily Eisbruch, Scott Haltzman, Alan Hurwitz, Jonathan Hutson, Vivian Levy, Laurie Pearlman, Joyce Reed, Maida Rogerson, Paul Roud, Lou Savary, Michael Shandler, Ervin Staub, Barbara Dafoe Whitehead, and Jonathan Wright.*

PREFACE

This book is about the heart, the universal symbol of caring and compassion—and specifically—how to keep the "heart" in marriage.

We wrote *The 5 Secrets of Marriage from the HEART* primarily for people whose marriage may not be going as well as they had hoped and are looking for ways to make it better. It is also meant for couples who are relating well and would like to grow even closer together. We also suggest practical ideas for friends and family members who are searching for ways to help and support a marriage in trouble.

Recent research confirms that children have a large stake in the health of their parents' marriage. The evidence is overwhelming that children do better, physically and emotionally, in a home with both parents present, except in cases of physical, emotional, and/or substance abuse. The current societal effort to strengthen the institution of marriage reflects the profound concern for how we are raising our children, who inevitably bear the brunt of our 43% national divorce rate.

Related research reveals a startling fact: 70% of couples who five years ago had rated their marriage "unhappy" or "very unhappy," are now reporting that they are "happy" or "very happy." This suggests that if couples are able to survive rough patches, they can develop a satisfying relationship. *The 5 Secrets of*

Marriage from the HEART offers a simple strategy to help couples get through these inevitable rough patches.

The two of us who wrote this book have been a married couple since 1977, and for the past eight years we have been partners in a couples education venture called "LoveWorks." Our commitment is to offer skills to couples to enrich their journey of committed partnership. Over the years, many participants in our workshops have suggested that the benefits of our ideas could be multiplied and magnified if we were to put them in a book.

Since we both prefer to teach by telling stories, we have allowed our guidance and suggestions to emerge from a fictional story. The book is a kind of parable, the tale of Donna and Bob Hartwell, whose relationship finds itself headed down a rough and rocky road. As this story took shape in our imagination, it forced us to sharpen and refine our understanding of what it truly takes to make a marriage work and, beyond that, what it takes to make it a daily blessing in the lives of both partners — and their children.

Our main desire is to show marital partners how much they themselves can do to make their relationship better and more satisfying, by applying the five basic HEART secrets, a powerful, practical way to strengthen marriages everywhere. With all our hearts, we hope that this story inspires you to take the journey.

CHAPTER 1

Unfaithful Anonymous

"My name is Bob, and I'm an unfaithful husband. Sort of. Well, not really. I didn't even do anything. At least Clinton got oral sex, and he didn't consider it having sex. I didn't even get that far. A couple of passionate kisses in an exotic setting and all of a sudden I'm a marital felon."

Half-smiling, Bob Hartwell looked around the room at the other fifteen people seated in a semi-circle on straight back chairs. All eyes were looking intently at him. Serious. Silent.

Bob thought to himself, "That opener would have drawn laughs from my American History class at the college. What's wrong with these people?"

But the others in the room sat stock still, waiting.

Bob was not happy to be there. The peculiar combination of resentment and embarrassment was coming out as a desire to entertain the group.

"My real crime was my stupidity: I told my wife."

He looked around for some kind of response.

Nothing, not even a nod. From anybody.

Nervously, he scratched his head. It was his turn to spill. He was on stage. Everyone waited, so he went on.

"If I had kept my big mouth shut, everything would have been fine. Well, maybe not fine, since my marriage wasn't all that great anyway, but at least I wouldn't be sleeping in the guest room and having to come here."

Bob considered himself a sort of amateur stand-up comic. His students were an especially appreciative and responsive audience. The classroom was his stage. But this was different.

"I'm here, by the way, courtesy of my wife's therapist, who supported my wife's paranoid characterization of my behavior as unfaithful."

Silence, still.

"Why did I go along with coming here, you ask? Two reasons: number one is Rocky, our ten-year-old son. I'll tell you, for me the sun rises and sets with that kid. He's fantastic—smart, funny, a great athlete—he loves baseball—and sweet-natured to boot." Bob smiled spontaneously as he pictured the last time he and Rocky had been tossing a baseball around in their back yard.

"There's no way I'm going to put up with seeing him every other weekend and half of vacations. Reason number two is even though things aren't great with us right now, I still love my wife. So here I am at, God help me, Unfaithful Anonymous."

UA was patterned on AA, Bob was told, but modified in format as a support group for unfaithful spouses. Bob had never been to an AA meeting or any other kind of support group where, as he imagined, you sat around, drank coffee and spilled your guts out in front of other people about your various addictions. As far as he was concerned, he wasn't a slave to any kind of addiction except the one where guys liked to look—just look—at pretty women. But, he thought, if that's an addiction, I have lots of good company.

He scanned the fifteen somber faces looking at him. He would hear some of their stories tonight, not all of them, but enough to convince him that he was out of place here with the rest, who were probably having torrid afternoon affairs with their female colleagues or their wives' best friends or clandestine meetings at midnight in dingy motels. The group was men only; there was a Women's Division that met separately. For obvious reasons, Bob thought.

The group waited, stone-faced.

"Donna is a piece of work. I met her in 1991 at a soccer banquet at the University. She got an award for being high scorer, as well as a varsity letter. A few years earlier, I had been a mid-fielder for the men's team. I saw her across the room and it was one of those magic things. She was tall, blond, graceful and utterly beautiful. I got up the nerve to walk over to her table. I introduced myself awkwardly and congratulated her. Then, miracle of miracles, she says, 'Let's get out of here and take a walk.' The rest was history.

"She was a senior, a marketing major in the business school, and I was a graduate student in American History, but we had other things in common. Like sports, movies, dancing. And great sex. Let us not forget that.

"After she graduated, we got married, and she supported me by selling real estate while I finished my doctorate. She was out every evening, but it didn't matter since I was doing my dissertation and could adjust my schedule to hers. By the way, my dissertation topic was 'Presidential Infidelity from Roosevelt to Johnson.' Pretty ironic, huh? Those guys should have come here. Except for Truman, they would have fit right in.

"After I got my doctorate, I was hired as an instructor at Wellington College and began my college teaching career. Now Donna's night and weekend work schedule began to pinch since my schedule was just the opposite, weekday mornings and afternoons. We began spending less time together.

"Then Rocky was born—Robert Jr. on his birth certificate—but he was kicking Donna in the womb so much she started referring to him as Rocky and it stuck. Rocky brought us back together for a while, but when she went back to work three months later and we split child care according to our schedules, it seemed like we had even less time together.

"One more little detail. After Rocky was born, our sex life took a nosedive. The combination of not much time and, on her part, not much interest, brought things to a near standstill. A graph of our sex frequency would look like the bear market of 2002. From two or three times a day before we were married, to daily while I was in graduate school, to two or three times a week before Rocky was born, to monthly if I'm lucky now. It's a good thing Rocky's such a great kid or I might resent him for costing me my sex life.

"Besides our infrequent sex, our lives were going in different directions. Donna gradually became a star residential real estate salesperson under the tutelage—are you ready for this?—of my mother. My mother had sold real estate and then bought the agency when the owner retired. When it became clear Donna was going to thrive in the field, my mom offered her a job and she accepted with the thought that eventually Donna would take over the operation. Her career was blossoming. She was earning more money than I was, a lot more.

"My life was centered on campus, the life of a scholar, an intellectual, and an assistant soccer coach. My friends were academics; hers were business people. The two groups didn't mix very well, and with the exception of our best friends Marvin and Sue, we argued over who to invite over for dinner and who to hang out with. So far, it's the normal marital conflicts of two very different people trying to build a life together and stumbling around and blaming each other for being so different. So how did I become the designated bad guy attending an Unfaithful Anonymous meeting?"

One guy on the extreme left, who looked like a plumber or a garage mechanic, coughed. Others turned to stare at him. Bob wondered if this guy had committed some serious breach of UA etiquette. For the most part, the rest of them seemed to Bob like figures in a wax museum, almost alive.

Bob looked down at his watch. He recalled how he was used to giving hour-long lectures effortlessly. Here, he was drained of energy after only three minutes into his 15 minutes in the UA spotlight.

But the show must go on, he thought, so he

entered into the formal confession of his crime.

"Well, every year the American Historical Association has an annual conference in some cushy locale where academics from all over the country get together. The ostensible purpose is to share new research findings and theories but just as important is networking for future employment, socializing and recreation. This year it was in San Antonio.

"Over the years, I have made many friends among the American historians who attend these conferences. One of my favorites is a Cuban-American woman from the University of Florida named Maritza. In addition to being a respected scholar, she happens to be drop-dead gorgeous—about five foot two, raven black hair, intense, cerebral, passionate. I don't believe in discriminating against attractive colleagues.

"Now Donna knew about this friendship and was not too thrilled about it. I think she picked up, with the radar that wives seem to have, that I was attracted to her, and not just to her intellectual gifts. But since it was strictly professional, there wasn't much she could say or do about it, except make occasional snide comments.

"Anyway, at the conference Maritza and I sat next to each other at a seminar on the history of American diplomacy in Cuba. After the seminar, we walked outside; it was a beautiful sunny day. Since we had some time before the next session, I proposed we take a picnic lunch and visit the Alamo, the famous site where in 1836 Americans fought to the last man against the Mexican army. While she picked up some sandwiches and a bottle of wine, I grabbed a blanket from my hotel room. We strolled over to the Alamo and found a quiet spot surrounded by foliage.

"After the lunch and the wine, I was feeling great. We talked about our careers and about our personal lives. She had recently broken up with an English professor, and I shared some of my recent marital woes. Inspired by the setting and the mood, I reached over and gave her a gentle hug. I was surprised when she looked up and kissed me lightly on the mouth. I kissed her back, this time a long, lingering, open-mouth delicious kiss with that great little body hugging me tightly. The next thing I knew we were lying together on the blanket, making out in earnest. A great moment, a wonderful connection. Academic conferences are not all boring.

"At that point, thoughts of my wife began to intrude, and I resolved—highly resolved, as Lincoln would have put it—not to carry this further. We got up, brushed ourselves off, and walked back to the conference, and that is the last time I saw Maritza, and I have had no contact with her since."

Like a good defense attorney in his closing remarks to the jury, he smiled as he scanned their faces. He waited for a few seconds. This time, he relished the silence. Then, dramatically, he softly spoke.

"So I ask you, was I unfaithful? Do I deserve to be sent off to Unfaithful Anonymous? Do I belong in a group with all of you who have tasted the fruits of adultery? My friend Marvin says I have the worst of both worlds: getting called unfaithful and not even getting laid."

Silence.

The group leader in a quiet but authoritative voice said, "Thank you, Bob."

As if roused from a trance, the group gave him

the same polite applause they accorded every speaker, regardless of what he said.

CHAPTER 2

Friend

With an angry forehand, Donna lashed at Sue's serve to the right corner, but she was slightly off balance when she swung, and she dumped the return into the net.

"Game and set," cried Sue, walking toward the side to pick up her towel. Sue Rogers was Donna Hartwell's closest friend.

"You killed me," said Donna, leaning over to pick up the tennis ball that had died in the net and was rolling back toward her.

"Some days the magic works, some days it doesn't," said Sue, slipping her racquet into her tennis bag.

"I couldn't get a first serve in the whole set," Donna lamented.

"I feel lucky when I can take a set from you," Sue replied, pleased with her victory but trying to be a gracious winner. They were walking side by side along the brick path up to the clubhouse.

"I couldn't keep my mind on the game," said Donna. "I kept thinking about Bob with that Cuban academic slut."

"What a shock that must have been!" Sue said. They walked a few steps in silence. Sue, a vibrant, petite woman with dark brown hair and dark brown eyes, looked small next to the much taller, strikingly blond woman. "Your Bob is the last guy I'd suspect of wandering."

"Not really," said Donna. "But I thought his womanizing period had ended before we were married."

"But he seems so devoted to you and Rocky."

"Well, I sure don't trust him now," said Donna with a quiet snort. "Three days away from home and he has a fling with a hot tamale. How devoted is that?"

Donna and Sue always drank a ritual glass of iced tea together on the clubhouse patio after their typical spirited singles match. Their iron chairs scraped on the tile floor as they pulled them out from the table to sit down.

When they had settled down with their iced teas, Sue leaned over toward Donna and asked the inevitable question. "Are you really thinking of divorcing him?"

"I don't know," said Donna with a sigh. "I feel so angry, so betrayed—humiliated, really. How could he do it? I know things weren't perfect between us. We both spend a lot of hours at work and most of our non-work time is centered around Rocky, but I didn't dream our marriage was in any danger."

Sue took a sip of her iced tea. As she set her glass down, she hesitated for a moment, took a breath, and tentatively said, "Marvin thinks you're giving him the electric chair for a misdemeanor."

Donna rolled her eyes and shook her head in disagreement. "Well, forgive me for maligning your dearly beloved, but Marvin's an idiot. Violating *my* trust is not a misdemeanor, and the way I feel now, if Bob weren't Rocky's father, flogging would be too good for him."

"I know you're upset," said Sue, "but truthfully, you've been complaining about Bob for years. As your friend, I've listened to plenty of rants about his shortcomings as a partner."

"Well," was all Donna could say, but Sue noticed that her friend didn't deny what she had just said.

"Look, I've got to run," said Sue rising from her chair. "Don't do anything rash," she said. "I'll call you tomorrow." Sue gave Donna a quick hug and walked through the clubhouse to the parking lot.

Donna remained sitting in deep contemplation, holding her iced tea glass with both hands. "What would it do to Rocky if we separated? It would shatter him. He worships Bob. Bob's his jokester buddy and baseball guru."

She felt deeply torn. Her chronic dissatisfaction with the marriage had been simmering at a low boil, and San Antonio had turned up the heat to full blast. Bob often seemed as if he were in a different world. Right now he was writing an article on the U.S. role in fomenting the Hungarian uprising of 1956. He was obsessed with ferreting out the evidence of false assurances of U.S. military assistance and oblivious to almost everything else, including Donna's daily melodrama of selling homes. He rarely asked her how her day had gone, and never expressed interest in her growing business.

She looked at her watch and realized she had just enough time to drive home, take a shower, dress for work, and meet her two o'clock client.

As she drove home, her mind was still stirring about her predicament and Bob's preoccupation with his professional article writing.

The one exception to Bob's obsession was Rocky's baseball career, she thought. Bob had played baseball with Rocky since he was old enough to walk and had recently taught him how to be a pitcher. Rocky was on a Little League team called the Rottweilers and was not only a pitcher but the team's best hitter. Donna was the one who drove Rocky to every practice, but Bob never missed a game. Father and son also went to a few Mets games together each year.

In her heart of hearts, Donna thought baseball was the most agonizingly boring game ever devised and, although careful not to disparage it, did not participate in the baseball mania that emanated from her husband and son.

Donna was not anti-sports. Far from it. She had been a star in college soccer, and after college she continued to run, including in 10K races, and play tennis. So she certainly understood the thrill of competition and striving for victory, but never having played baseball herself and never having been enrolled in the baseball culture by her father or brother, its leisurely 19th century charms were utterly lost on her.

As she pulled into their driveway, she wondered what it would do to Rocky's spirit to be separated from his baseball guru/dad, not to have it nourished everyday at breakfast as they celebrated or suffered together with the Mets.

Donna got out of her car and went into the house, feeling truly miserable. "What do I do now?" she wondered. "Where do we go from here?"

CHAPTER 3

Buddies

Sue's husband Marvin was Bob's closest friend. He was in the political science department at Wellington, so he was a colleague as well as a friend. Just as Sue was ending her post-tennis visit with Donna in the bright, warm sunlight, Bob wandered over to Marvin's office, where the window air conditioner was grinding away.

Marvin was a tall, lanky man with brown curly hair receding in the front and warm, sometimes mischievous eyes. With his long legs draped over his desk, he looked like the former basketball player he, in fact, was.

"Hey, sport. Hope I'm not interrupting anything important," Bob said as he stuck his head in the office.

"Naw, just grading some semi-literate papers on Clinton's impeachment." Marvin lifted a handful of student papers and waved them at Bob as evidence. "Half the students are appalled at Clinton's stupidity, and the other half think Paula Jones should be burned as a witch and maybe Ken Starr along with her. Come on in and sit down. How was Unfaithful Anonymous?"

Bob sat down in the wooden chair, the only horizontal space not cluttered with books and articles. "It was actually fascinating in a bizarre sort of way, but I don't belong there. Donna and I have lots of problems, but adultery isn't one of them. I'm not clear why she even wanted me to go."

"You want to hear my theory?" asked Marvin, as he swiveled on his chair. He waited.

"Sure," Bob finally said. "Go ahead."

Still gazing at his diploma wall, Marvin brought his two hands together so that just his fingertips touched each other. "Well," he began, "some people, the Catholic Church for example, believe there's no penance without penitence, so for the sin of wandering off the marital reservation, instead of ten Hail Marys, you're being sentenced to an indeterminate term of Unfaithful Anonymous."

For a moment, Bob pondered Marvin's sacramental analogy, then said, "Aside from the fact that Donna's not Catholic, I don't see how it's going to help anything."

"Well, it's necessary but probably not sufficient," Marvin added with a logical twist. "It's a gesture you're going to have to make, but you're going to have to come up with more gestures."

"Is that the Marvin Rogers Gesture Theory of Marriage?" asked Bob, smiling.

"As a matter of fact, it is. Walt Whitman once

said: 'My words are nothing, my gestures everything.'"

"Like, what kind of gestures are you talking about?"

"Well, let's see" said Marvin, stroking his chin and turning toward Bob. "Flowers are always nice. A dinner out at a nice place. Or better yet, you cook a special dinner, serve it with candlelight and wine, and arrange a sleep-over for Rocky at a friend's house."

Bob shook his head to reject each of Marvin's suggestions. "Right now, I'm so deep in Donna's dog house, I'm not sure she'd show up." He rose from his chair and began to move about the room nervously. "I don't know what to do. I mean, she's out every night and most weekend days showing houses to prospects. Then she gets all self-righteous and injured when I show a little interest in a woman who, among her other attributes, as least had the virtue, unlike my wife, of being in the same place with me at the same time." Bob turned to face Marvin directly. "That's the Bob Hartwell Propinquity Theory of Marriage."

"Propinquity? What does that mean?"

"It means closeness," said Bob with intensity. He emphasized the following words by hammering on Marvin's desk. "It means you can't be emotionally close unless you're physically close, and you can't be physically close if you're out peddling real estate at all hours." Bob realized he was almost shouting.

"So what are you going to do?"

"I don't know," said Bob, dropping himself back into the chair with a deep sigh. "It's a little late to order our wives back to the bedroom and kitchen."

"About two generations too late," added Marvin.

"Besides, my mother is Donna's partner and

mentor," said Bob.

"Oh, right. That's a complication." Marvin began fidgeting with a pencil. "What do your parents have to say about all this?"

"I'm about to find out," said Bob. "I'm going over there tomorrow."

"That should be interesting." Marvin unwound his legs from the desk and got up. "Let me know how it goes, buddy."

CHAPTER 4

Rocky

At 3:30 Rocky bounded in with the screen door slamming behind him. A wiry kid with bright narrow eyes, light brown hair and a ready smile, he bore a slight resemblance to Howdy Doody. He ran upstairs—he never seemed to just walk anywhere—and shouted, "Hey, Mom, anyone home?"

Donna emerged from the bathroom. The sound of her son's voice always seemed to buoy her spirits. She responded, matching his excited tone. "Hey, Rocks, how was school?"

"Okay. I got an A- on the geography test." He knew parents were always interested in school and liked to hear about his academic progress. But then he moved onto what really mattered "I gotta get ready for the game."

Pitching for the Rottweilers in the Little League

for 10–11 year olds was the most exciting part of his life. He loved baseball, he loved competition, and he especially loved being the star of the team, which he definitely was. Today's game was against their biggest cross-town rival, the Stingers, who were currently occupying first place in the league. Rocky quickly shed his school clothes and donned the blue and white uniform of the Rottweilers, feeling like Clark Kent transforming himself into Superman.

"Is Dad going to be there?" he yelled to his mom downstairs.

"Oh, I'm sure your father would never miss something as important as a baseball game," Donna replied coolly.

Although Rocky was running downstairs as she spoke, he could not miss the edge in her voice. He asked, "Are you ticked off at Dad, or something?"

"Why do you ask?"

"I don't know—just the way you said it."

Donna experienced a deep pang. She was at pains to hide from Rocky the anger she was feeling toward her husband and wanted desperately for Rocky to be protected from their marital problems.

"No," she said off-handedly, "I just said he'd be there, and I'm sure he will." Donna resolved to be even more careful about how she spoke about Bob in Rocky's presence. "That kid has an antenna that won't quit," she thought to herself. "He picks up everything."

The sky was overcast and threatening as they drove to the local baseball field.

"Gee, I hope we don't get rained out," Rocky said.

His mother replied, "It doesn't look too promising."

When they arrived, the Stingers were taking

batting practice, and everyone was anxiously peering up at the ominous sky.

Bob was parking his car near the ball field when he noticed the first drops of rain beginning to fall on his windshield. The players, coaches, parents and assorted family members began to notice the rain, too. The two coaches huddled briefly and emerged declaring a rain-out and postponement. The groans of the young players were audible, but as the rain gathered force, everyone ran for the parking lot.

Bob stood outside his car and looked around. When he saw that Rocky was with his mother, he yelled over to them, "I'll see you at home."

Rocky ran over to his father, as Donna proceeded to her own car. Rocky yelled back to his mom, "I'm going with Dad."

Donna said stiffly, "I'll see you at home." With her hair and clothes already damp with rain, she felt a flash of anger as she got into her car. She slammed her car door shut and drove off.

Rocky got into his Dad's car. As soon as he closed the door, he asked, "Is Mom mad at us, do you think?"

"Probably not at you. More likely just at me." Like Donna, Bob was treading lightly here, walking the tightrope of not saying too much but also not wanting to lie to his son.

"So, why at you, Dad? Did you leave the kitchen messy again?"

"Yeah, maybe I did," Bob responded, glad to be able to validate a rather benign interpretation. But he also knew that Rocky had begun to sense the coolness and distance in his parents' relationship. Messy kitchen theories would not survive for long unless something changed soon.

When they arrived home, Donna's car was already in the garage. They ran in the house, getting semi-drenched, and Rocky ran upstairs to get out of his uniform. Bob found Donna in the kitchen preparing a chicken casserole.

"You can heat this up for dinner for yourself and Rocky," she said. "I'll be out showing some houses."

"Couldn't you have dinner with us and schedule the clients for later? It would be nice to be together as a family."

"Yes, it would be nice," she said with that edge in her voice, "but no, it's not possible. This couple is close to bidding on a house, and I have to be there when they're available or they'll find someone else who is."

Feeling chastened and rejected by her response, Bob changed the subject. "Too bad about the rainout today. Aside from Rocky's disappointment, I played hooky on a departmental meeting."

"Not a good move in your campaign for tenure, I would think."

"Probably not, but Rocky's games come first," Bob said, feeling defensive.

Having been an assistant professor for four years and published a book and a series of articles in professional journals, Bob was eligible to apply for tenure this year and had done so, but with the college experiencing a financial squeeze, tenure was not a sure thing.

Donna kept working at the kitchen counter, making more movements and noise than were needed, never looking directly at Bob, even when she spoke to him. Walking away from him toward the pantry, she commented, "If you don't get tenure, they give you one year and then you're out on the street. With that hanging over us, I don't think I'll neglect any prospects. You might consider how your department colleagues might feel about being stiffed."

Bob reacted strongly, "Damn it, Donna, it's not the same, and you know it. Half the department skips those meetings." He wanted to walk over to her and shake some sense into her. At least make her look him in the face. Instead, he stood in the center of the kitchen, feeling helpless, and gave out a big sigh. Then he said quietly but with conviction, "I'll handle the tenure, but it won't be at the expense of missing Rocky's baseball games."

Donna was not about to let Bob have the last word. "Well, you can rant all you want, but it won't make a difference if you end up with a big thumbs down." And then, in clipped tones, still not looking at him, she said dismissively, "I've got to go. I should be back before Rocky goes to bed."

She put on her raincoat, grabbed her umbrella, and walked through the doorway to the garage without saying goodbye.

When he heard her car engine start, he looked toward the garage and said to an empty kitchen in a sad, slow voice, "And it was wonderful to be with you too, dear."

CHAPTER 5

Anger

Ever since Rocky had gone upstairs to bed at nine, Bob had been pacing the living room preparing what he wanted to say to Donna. He rehearsed a dozen different ways of starting the conversation he knew needed to happen. They had to break this stony, cold impasse in their relationship. He couldn't stand it anymore. And he felt Donna wasn't going to be the one to take the first step toward reconciliation. Planning his side of the case felt reminiscent of his high school debate team preparations. On his fingers he counted arguments, pro and con. He tried out some words, spoken to the fireplace. Nothing seemed quite the right way to approach her. The more he thought about their current situation, the more upset he got.

It was ten o'clock when he heard the garage door begin its familiar grind and the sound of Donna's car pulling in. She would come in through the kitchen, so he began walking there to meet her, perhaps even to confront her.

As he came into the scene of their last encounter, the kitchen's fluorescent lights seemed especially harsh. He looked over at the sink and the counter to see that he had done a good job of cleaning up his and Rocky's supper dishes. He must remember to thank her for preparing supper for them.

Donna entered quietly. She was surprised to see Bob in the kitchen. "Is he asleep?" she asked.

"I think so," Bob replied. "How did it go?"

"They're still thinking about it." She put her coat and umbrella away.

She hadn't scored a sale tonight, he realized, and she didn't sound very hopeful. He wanted to go over and hold her, reassure her that she would do great tomorrow and hook a big fish, but he knew that she would rebuff any form of touch. He remembered the chicken casserole.

"By the way, thanks for a nice dinner," he said, smiling. "Rocky and I ate most of it, but there's a little left in the refrigerator, if you're hungry."

"You're welcome, and no thank you," she said without any emotion.

Bob mustered his courage, cleared his throat, and said, "Donna, I'd like to talk about our situation."

Donna took a cookie from the plate on the counter and sat down at the kitchen table. "Talk away," she said as she nibbled.

Bob was too nervous to sit. Adrenaline was pumping through his veins. He took a deep breath and plunged in. "This isn't working for me. I went to the session at Unfaithful Anonymous and it was ridiculous—I didn't belong there." His hands were gesturing almost passionately, as he paced the kitchen. "We're co-existing here like it's the Cold War. We live like housemates rather than as husband and wife. No kind words, no affectionate pats. Not to mention sex. I hate it. I hate sleeping in the guestroom. I hate walking on tiptoe all the time, afraid I'll say something to set you off. We're not getting anywhere. I don't know what you want, except maybe to punish me."

Donna frowned while he was talking. As far as she was concerned, the issue under discussion wasn't at all about her, it was about him, unfaithful Bob. "No, Bob," she spoke with resignation and frustration, the way you talk to a child when he refuses to get your point. "You do belong there. Unfaithful Anonymous is exactly where you belong. But you don't get it. You think you have to go to bed with someone to be unfaithful. Well, you're wrong. It's much easier than that to break faith. You're in the guestroom because right now I can't stand the thought of sleeping in the same room with you. And believe me, I don't feel the least affectionate towards you. I'm angry at you and I don't know when that will change."

She got up and walked to the refrigerator and opened the door. She was about to look in, but turned to him and self-righteously spat out, "Maybe you should have thought about that before you had your little picnic." Then, she put her head back behind the refrigerator door, dismissing him.

"Donna, that is just rampant bull. You're using that non-event to cover all the other stuff, the stuff we never talk about, how our lives are going off in different directions. When do we ever get to talk about the real stuff?"

Donna closed the refrigerator door, studied an apple she had taken from the fruit bin, and acted as though she had not heard a word Bob had said. "Look, I'm tired from showing houses," she said, "and I don't see this conversation getting anywhere. I'm going to bed."

She walked briskly out of the kitchen as she took a first bite out of her apple.

Bob, stunned by her departure, just sat there and shook his head. He wondered whether this was how marriages ended. Were they headed towards divorce?

He shivered.

"This can't be happening," he said aloud. "What should I do? Where can I go for help?"

CHAPTER 6

Harry

Bob Hartwell described his father Harry as "quite a guy," but that was an understatement. Harry had been a star fullback at Duke and then followed his own father into the oil business ending up as head of Ramoco's oil refining operations for the entire USA, before retiring three years ago. Since then, Harry and Molly, Bob's mother, who was semi-retired from her real estate agency, had dedicated themselves to various charitable causes, such as driving for Meals on Wheels every Tuesday.

At Ramoco, in the early part of his career, Harry had the reputation of an autocratic, demanding boss—a holy terror to his intimidated employees, who had given him the nickname "The Abominable No-Man." As a father, Harry, although devoted to his son, had been a strict disciplinarian, going so far as to refuse to pay Bob's college tuition after a semester when his grades fell below a 2.5 GPA.

But then something happened that had caused a remarkable change. Harry had a heart attack, and during his convalescence and recovery appeared to mellow. He was more soft-spoken, kinder with Molly, more patient and understanding with Bob, and a more compassionate boss to his refinery staff. At that time, Bob, being a typically self-absorbed college student, didn't really take the time to find out what had caused the change. He assumed it was his father's brush with mortality. Mostly, he just enjoyed finally having a father he could approach and talk to and share things with without being judged or put down.

After his heart attack, Harry had become Bob's friend as well as his father. In fact, when Bob and Donna were married, Bob was thrilled to have Harry agree to stand up as his best man. As a gift, Bob had a gold tie bar engraved for Harry that read: "For Harry, my old man and my best man. With love."

As Bob pulled into his parents' driveway, he noticed his father working in the back yard. Harry had developed a new hobby after retirement, an unlikely one for a former fullback: growing roses. The older man was kneeling in earth still wet from yesterday's rain, busily engaged in pruning his prized rose bushes, as Bob walked over and squeezed his father's shoulders from behind.

"Hi, Dad, how are the rosies doing?"

Harry got up, turned around, and smiled to see his son.

Bob spontaneously hugged him. "I'm going to get you all wet," his father replied, yet pleased that his son was willing to hug him despite his sweaty condition. "What's new in academia?"

"Not much. I'm still trying to figure out who promised what to the Hungarians in '56—it's for an article. Where's Mom?"

"She's out doing errands. She should be back soon. Rocky get rained out yesterday?"

"Yeah. He was so hyped. I felt sorry for him. But he gets to learn that rainouts are a part of life."

"Ain't that the truth. Come on in. I'll buy you a beer." Harry put down his pruning sheers, and they walked to the house and entered the door to their screened-in porch, where Ram, his Tibetan terrier, was waiting with tail vigorously wagging. Harry, who had never previously liked pets, especially around the house, got Ram shortly after he finished his convalescence from the heart attack. It was love at first sight for both Harry and Ram. Named after Ramoco, Ram had become a beloved member of the Hartwell household, and was forever at Harry's heels whenever his master was at home.

Bob plopped down heavily on the couch, while Harry went into the kitchen to get their beers, followed by Ram. He came back with two Heinekens, handed one to Bob, and sat down in a chair next to the couch, so they could easily look at one another.

Ram jumped into Harry's lap, his privileged spot, and looked into Harry's eyes, as if to say, "Is my being here right now okay with you?" Harry stroked the dog assuring him that he was welcome to remain there.

After a moment of savoring the cold brew, Harry observed, "You're looking a bit bedraggled, Bob.

Anything wrong?"

"Well, funny you should ask, Dad. Physically, I'm healthy as a horse, but otherwise, I'm a solid mess. Other than that I'm fine," Bob said trying to make light of his distress.

"Anything you want to talk about with the old man?" Harry offered, looking directly at Bob.

"Well, I don't know. Do you have experience in how to fix screwed up marriages?"

Harry chuckled softly. "I certainly should. I had to fix mine a few years ago, and we've made it through forty-three years."

"You and Mom had problems? I never knew that."

"If you consider my being an inconsiderate bully a problem, yeah, I guess you could say we had problems. Molly sort of put up with me. She learned how to not take my bluster too seriously, how to operate around me. And most amazing, she loved me in spite of all that. Your mother is a remarkable woman."

"Amen to that." Bob nodded his wholehearted agreement. "I'll drink to her any day," he added, lifting his bottle and taking a sip of his beer. Harry did the same, then continued.

"But despite her tolerance, or maybe even because of it, I had to learn to be a better partner, more accepting and more appreciative of all the things she does for me. It was a hard lesson for an old bull like me."

Bob proceeded to give his dad the highlights of his current marital situation. Harry listened attentively, shaking his head at various points. Bob felt understood by his father, and that made it easier to share more details as well as his feelings.

"Sounds like you are indeed in the soup, son.

I'd be willing to share the strategy I used to change if you're interested in hearing it."

"Of course I'm interested. Frankly, even I noticed how much you changed after your heart attack, but I never had any inkling how you did it."

"Well, all the doctors were telling me I had to change or I would surely have more heart attacks and die. Naturally, that kind of got my attention. I knew that I was a Type A on steroids and that my interpersonal style was aggressive to the point of bullying. I had heard some feedback, including my Abominable nickname, but chose to ignore it. Lying there in the hospital, I also became aware of how isolated and alone I was, and it made me feel a great sadness. With my life possibly on the line, I began to think for the first time, not about what I wanted from others, but about what they might want from me. I did a lot of thinking during those days. That's when I had a major insight about relating to others."

"What was that, Dad?" asked Bob, surprised that his father had this introspective turn of mind.

"It dawned on me that we—everyone—are always making requests of one another. I thought of one request that we all make, then another, then another. Soon I had uncovered five of these universal requests. I call them universal because we're all always making them to one another. Sometimes these requests are made verbally, but mostly they remain unspoken. But they are sincere requests nonetheless. In the end, I realized that everyone was making five unspoken requests not only of me but also of everyone else, and that if I honored those requests, they would feel respected and even cared about. I realized that if I devoted my efforts to honoring their unspoken requests, it would change all my relationships, including most significantly, my relationship with myself. I would no longer be killing myself charging after my various agendas, and I would no longer feel so isolated and alone."

Bob was listening, transfixed by his father's story. He had a hundred questions but settled on one. "What did you do?"

Harry shook his head and smiled. "I wish I could tell you it was a straight line from point A to point B, but there were bumps in the road. Mainly, my resistance to change. As you know, I'm not too fond of change, so at first I was depressed and then resentful, but eventually it sunk in that it was either change or die. I was not ready to cash in my chips."

"Five unspoken requests," Bob said. "I've never heard of anything like that."

"Neither had I. It's like these unspoken requests are flying under the radar of our awareness. Nobody seems to know about them. That's why I think of them as the Five Secrets."

"Now you've got me really intrigued," Bob said. "I assume you're going to tell me what they are."

"I certainly am. I created the acronym HEART to help me remember them. Here, let me show you."

With that Harry lifted Ram off his lap, took out his wallet, opened it, and looked for something. In a moment, he took out a small card the size of a business card and handed it to Bob. "Here are the five HEART secrets all written down for you."

THE *5* SECRETS
OF MARRIAGE FROM THE HEART

Hear and understand me.

Even if you disagree, please don't make me wrong.

Acknowledge the greatness within me.

Remember to look for my loving intentions.

Tell me the truth with compassion.

"Those are the five. All the changes you noticed in my relationship with Mom and with you were based on my efforts to honor what I believe were her unspoken requests of me, and yours as well."

Bob sat silently, taking all this in. He never imagined that there was a system behind his father's mellowing. He was dumbfounded by the thought that identifying five unspoken requests could motivate drastic change in his behavior. "Dad, wasn't it terribly hard for you to change the way you were with everyone in your life? You'd been such a tough customer for so long."

"Yes, it was hard, but I believed that my life depended on it. It occurs to me in your case that maybe your marriage depends on it."

"You could be right," said Bob, getting up and walking around nervously. "But how do I undo the Alamo using the HEART secrets?"

"You can't re-write history, son. But I have a hunch that, for Donna, the Alamo incident was the culmination, not the beginning, of the problem and that integrating the HEART secrets could make a difference."

CHAPTER 7

The First Unspoken Request

Bob was squirming on the couch. He was intrigued by the idea that Donna, despite her hostile behavior, could be still making these unspoken requests of him. With a puzzled look, he turned to his father. "Dad, could you say a little more about each of the five requests and how you go about honoring them? I mean, Donna is downright hostile to me these days. Is she still, as you say, making these five requests of me? Today?"

"Sure she is, son. She's making them today, tomorrow, and the next day. We all make them of one another every day." Harry leaned forward in his chair and looked right at Bob. "You're making them to me right this minute. And I'm making them to you. Everybody is making them to everyone else all the time."

Bob was also leaning forward, intent on

catching every word.

"In your case," began his father, "the meaning and importance of that card I gave you would be clearer if it had a subtitle that read *five unspoken requests of each spouse to the other,* so keep that new subtitle in mind as we talk."

Bob nodded his head in agreement.

"Let's start with the first one, HEAR AND UNDERSTAND ME," Harry began. "This secret expresses everyone's deep desire to have their thoughts and feelings fully taken in by their listener, especially I might add, when that listener is your spouse or intimate partner. Now, I used to think I was a great listener. In fact, I thought I was so good that I knew what Molly was going to say before she finished her sentences, so rather than waste her time and mine, I would interrupt her and tell her what she was thinking. And then I was surprised when she got annoyed."

Bob laughed. "You used to do that to me, too."

"In your mother's case, what I learned is that for her to feel fully heard and understood, I needed to provide evidence that I had received the message she intended to send. I first learned to hold my tongue until she finished her thought. Then, instead of simply disagreeing with her or offering my opinion of the situation, I discovered I first had to respond to what she had said by giving her a kind of listening check or summary. To do the check, I would say things like, 'Right now, you're feeling . . . ' or 'Basically, your idea here is to . . . ' Then if she nodded her head, I knew I had gotten it right. This change alone made a huge difference."

Bob nodded his head. "I can relate to that. As

one of your former favorite interruptees."

His father chuckled. "I'm glad you said former. Molly claimed that in our first 30 years of marriage, she hardly got to finish a sentence. A slight exaggeration maybe but, when I started practicing that first secret, HEAR AND UNDERSTAND ME, she sure noticed the difference and appreciated it."

"Well," said Bob, "I understand it, but I don't know if I could actually do it, especially with Donna. Whenever she attacks me verbally, I want to defend myself. I don't feel like doing a listening check, as you describe it. I want to fight back. And, sometimes, I just want to run away from her anger."

"You understand the first secret theoretically, but you're not sure you could put it into practice?" asked his father.

Bob nodded.

"And you'd rather fight with her or flee from her anger, rather than stand there and summarize what she just said to you?"

"Exactly," said Bob.

"Did you notice," said his father, "that I just practiced the first secret with you? I showed you that I was listening to you and understood you. And you confirmed that you were heard and understood by me."

"Yes," agreed Bob, "but I wasn't angry at you or making accusations the way Donna does to me. It's a very different situation."

"You feel there is a big difference in practicing it when you're with someone who's calm and rational, than when you're with someone who's highly emotional?" his father asked, another listening check.

"You bet I do," said Bob. He was up again, and

began pacing back and forth. From Harry's lap, Ram's eyes followed Bob as he moved around the porch.

"Let me ask you a question, Bob," Harry began. "Does Donna begin shooting her verbal pistols at you the moment you walk in the door?"

"Not really," said Bob. "It usually takes a little while before she warms to the task."

"Well, maybe if you start practicing hearing and understanding soon after you come in the door, her level of anger might not get a chance to escalate. Often, people get angry precisely because their unspoken request to be heard and understood is rejected right from the get-go."

"That makes sense," admitted Bob, "but I'm not sure I could stand there simply reflecting what she says. I'm not accustomed to doing that kind of dialogue."

"Are you telling me that professors are more used to giving their opinions and ideas than listening to those of others?"

Bob laughed. "Sort of, I guess, but not exactly."

"Help me to understand what you're trying to say," Harry said. "Tell me what having a dialogue or conversation means to you."

"It means that two people share their ideas and feelings with one another," said Bob, as if this should be obvious.

"Well," asked his father, "what happens in a dialogue after I share my ideas and you share yours? Is there a further step in the process? Do they each say to the other, 'You're right'?"

"For me, I would certainly want the other person to say that in response to my ideas," said Bob.

"Then," asked his father, "do you think the

other person would want you to do the same for his or her ideas?"

"Sure," Bob admitted.

"But what if you don't agree with the other person?" asked Harry.

"I'd try to convince him that I was right," said Bob.

"And what if the other person tried to convince you that he or she was right?"

"Then, we'd have a debate on our hands," said Bob.

"Is that what happens between you and Donna?" Harry asked his son. "Does your dialogue often turn into debate?"

"Sure," admitted Bob. "And I enjoy winning debates."

"And what does winning a debate do for you?" Harry asked.

"I feel good about it," said Bob.

"And how do you think Donna feels whenever you win?"

"Defeated, I guess." At that moment, Bob stopped and gave his father an embarrassed look. "I think I've just said that I like to score points in my marriage and win the game whenever I can."

"That's what I heard you saying, son," said Harry. "I just wanted to make sure I was hearing right. To do it, I kept practicing the first secret. I kept hearing and understanding you. I didn't challenge you or debate you. I didn't disrespect a word you said. We kept a dialogue going. The question now is: How central to your definition of a good marriage is scoring debate points against your spouse?"

"Dad, I love Donna with all my heart." He was pleading for understanding.

"What I hear you saying is that with your heart you love Donna, but with your intellect and your behavior you tend to see Donna as an opponent in a sporting game." Then Harry asked him, "Am I hearing you correctly?"

"Dad," he replied quietly, "I can't say no. The way you characterized my attitude toward Donna and our marriage is pretty sad, but pretty close to true."

"I also hear you saying that you really wish that you could get your behavior to follow the love that's in your heart," said his father. "Is that right?"

"Well . . . yeah, I guess," admitted Bob. "But how do you do that? I mean, habits are habits and if Donna doesn't change, how can I be expected to change?"

"It's not about expectations—it's about what you want. In my case, I wanted to keep living. In your case, you're deciding whether saving your marriage is worth changing some of your ways of relating. But essentially, I had to do the same as you would have to do with Donna."

"What's that, Dad?" Bob asked.

"It's all on that little card I gave you—everything you need in order to get your behavior lined up with your heart's deepest desires."

CHAPTER 8

The Second Unspoken Request

Bob was looking down at his fingernails but not seeing them. In his mind, picturing himself in a dialogue with Donna, he was calmly listening to her and reflecting back to her what she was saying to him.

He was jolted out of his reverie when Ram jumped from Harry's lap and ran to the screen door, where he stood, tail wagging and eyes focused on Harry.

"Looks like Ram thinks it's time for us to step outside," Harry said. "He probably wants to honor his natural needs."

Harry stood up and with a twist of his head toward the door beckoned Bob to join him. As the two men stood, Ram's grateful tail began wagging even more intensely than before.

"We hear and understand you, Ram," said Bob with a chuckle.

As soon as Harry opened the screen door, Ram bounded into the yard and ran over to his favorite tree. When he finished, he ran back to Harry and waited expectantly at his feet. Harry bent down to scratch the back of Ram's neck, saying to him, "Let's see if Bob is as ready for a little exercise as you seem to be."

"Sure, Dad," answered Bob. "Maybe we can talk a bit about the second secret on your card?" From his shirt pocket he took the card his father had given him and read aloud, "The second one is EVEN IF YOU DISAGREE, PLEASE DON'T MAKE ME WRONG."

"This one has to do with blaming and put-downs," began Harry. They walked alongside his flower garden on the flat stepping-stones Harry had arranged there to keep shoes dry when the earth was damp as it was today. "When I was upset with Molly," Harry continued, "I would insult her intelligence. When we disagreed, I would discredit her competence in order to win an argument. When something went wrong, I would find a way to blame her and make it somehow her fault. In other words, I would make her the problem. Naturally, as you might imagine, this didn't go over too big. It didn't endear me to her—it just pushed her away."

"I must have picked up some of those old habits of yours, Dad," said Bob,"because I am good at disagreeing, insulting, and blaming—especially Donna.

"But you know, Dad, there are times when Donna is wrong, like when she criticizes me for spending too much time at the library and then puts me down for missing a faculty meeting so I can go watch Rocky play baseball. What do you do then?"

"Your mother and I still disagree at times, because we're both strong and independent people, but now I try to do it with great respect. Besides, your mother is highly intelligent and competent—why pretend otherwise?—and so, by the way, is your wife." He looked over at Bob to make sure he agreed with his appraisal of his son's wife.

"Donna's doing a fantastic job with the real estate agency," said Bob. "I know that, Dad. The problem is with us, her and me."

"So, anyway," Harry continued, turning to look directly at Bob, "if you want to manage your marriage according to those HEART secrets," Harry began counting on his fingers, "put-downs, name-calling, and insults are off limits from now on."

"What do you do when a put-down reply or an insult is right on the tip of your tongue?" asked Bob.

"Occasionally," said Harry, "I have to bite my tongue, but it's worth it."

"What if Donna starts insulting and blaming me?"

"Simple," replied his father. "You practice the first HEART secret. You show her that you are hearing and understanding her, what she's thinking and feeling. But by no means does her outburst give you permission to fight back. Put-downs, name-calling, insults and blaming are out of bounds for you."

"You know, Dad, those rules are not very fair," said Bob. "If your opponent has a sword, you need to have one, too."

"Marriage is not a sword fight, Bob, it's teamwork. You and Donna are on the same side. These HEART secrets will help you turn your marriage from a winner-take-all battle into an everybody-wins invest-ment. If you keep making Donna wrong when you dis-agree with her, you put your marriage into a tailspin.

"But I'm so good at insults and name-calling, Dad."

"Unfortunately, son, you learned it from a master—me. I hope you can unlearn from me, too."

"I'm sure I can, Dad, but I think I'll have to restate the second HEART secret to: *When in doubt, bite your tongue.*"

They both laughed.

CHAPTER 9

The Third Unspoken Request

The two men were walking along the fence at the rear of the property. Ram was happily running to and fro, delighted to be loose and free. "Look at those roses, Bob. Aren't they beautiful?" Harry bent over to grasp one of the blossoms and smelled it.

"You really love those flowers, don't you, Dad?"

"If you take a look at the HEART card in your pocket, I'm sort of practicing the third unspoken request."

Bob reached for the HEART card and read: ACKNOWLEDGE THE GREATNESS WITHIN ME.

"By focusing my whole attention on this rose, admiring it and smelling it," Harry said, "I am acknowledging its greatness."

"What has that got to do with Donna and me?"

"Everyone has some special talents or qualities,

and we all walk around hoping somebody will notice. Acknowledging strengths is like watering a tender plant—it helps it grow."

"So, not only do I have to be understanding and show that I'm listening carefully to her every word," Bob began, "but I also have to go unarmed into every encounter with her, forbidden to kick, scream or fight back. And now, you're telling me I have to sing her praises while she is verbally assaulting me? Come on, Dad." Bob threw his arms into the air with an uneasy laugh. "I'm a good guy, but I'm not Gandhi."

"In my marriage, before my heart attack," said Harry, looking off into the distance as if remembering an old familiar scene, "I would say my ratio of criticisms to praise at work or at home was much the same, probably around ten to one. This principle says the ratio should be exactly the opposite, at least 4 or 5 acknowledgements to any one bit of criticism. How's your ratio?"

Bob frowned, "Not so good, I'm afraid. Donna's so darn organized and competent that I actually have to look for things to pick at, if I want to try to cut her down to size, which is my usual practice. She would be shocked or think I was ill if I started acknowledging her greatness to her face."

"That's a wife's usual response to un-asked-for praise. Molly was pretty surprised, too, when I started dropping words of appreciation on her, but you can be sure it was a pleasant surprise."

"I'll bet it was," said Bob, "but where do I start with Donna?"

"Just a few moments ago you told me that Donna was very organized and competent. Those words came out of your mouth, except you saw those points of greatness as something keeping you from getting your way. You were blaming her greatness for your problems."

"It sounds pretty dumb when you put it that way," admitted Bob.

"Acknowledging the greatness in your partner always strengthens your marriage. It can't fail to do that."

"But, how do I do it when Donna and I are in the middle of an argument?"

"Well, that's difficult, for sure. First of all, if you're honoring the first two unspoken requests from the start, you'll be having fewer arguments. Second, if you're in an argument, honoring those requests will tend to defuse it and lower the emotional temperature. It may never escalate into a real fight. Third, when the storm passes, the sunlight returns, and I've found that's the perfect time to acknowledge greatness."

"But I like to fight," said Bob with great emphasis. "It makes me feel alive."

"Encouraging competitive anger is like taking drugs." Harry mimicked an addict putting a needle in his arm and squeezing the syringe. "It may give you a short-lived high, but the letdown is terrible, and the long-term cost to your health is extremely high."

"You mean that when I win an argument or succeed in putting Donna down, I might feel a momentary boost to my ego, but, long term, I'm crippling my marriage?"

"Exactly," said Harry, "and believe me, winning a fight with your spouse is the Booby Prize. The real prize is enjoying peace, love and harmony. Look, Ram is back near the screen door. I guess he's had enough running around for a while. Maybe we could discuss the last two unspoken requests on the porch."

"Good idea."

"Another beer?"

"Sure."

CHAPTER 10

The Fourth Unspoken Request

After Harry handed his son a bottle and put his own on the table beside his chair, Ram jumped into Harry's lap. Harry's hand automatically began petting the terrier, as he said to Bob, "Okay. Moving right along. Read the fourth request for us."

"You know what it says, Dad, don't you?"

"Of course," his father said, smiling. Then, in a proud voice, he recited, "It says REMEMBER TO LOOK FOR MY LOVING INTENTIONS." Turning to Bob, he said, "I asked you to read it because I want you to hear yourself saying it."

"You have all five requests memorized?"

"Sure," said Harry. "Almost always after I have a meeting with someone, I do what I call a HEART Check. I recall all five unspoken requests and ask myself how many of them I fulfilled in that meeting. The

HEART Check is my way of keeping me on my toes in my relationships. It's amazing how easy it is to slip back into old destructive habits."

"I'll have to learn how to do a HEART Check," said Bob, "but first explain the fourth unspoken request."

"This is an elementary one." Harry repeated the request. "REMEMBER TO LOOK FOR MY LOVING INTENTIONS. When you think about it," said Harry looking at his son, "does Donna get up in the morning, look into the mirror and think: 'How can I screw things up for Bob today?'"

"Recently, maybe." Bob laughed. "No, of course she doesn't."

"Of course not," Harry agreed. "She's out there doing her best every day. Her best as Rocky's mother, her best at selling real estate and even, I bet, her best as your wife. So, if she's doing her best, even if something goes wrong, it's both accurate and fair to acknowledge her positive intention, even if the results weren't great."

"I guess you're right," admitted Bob.

"And better yet," Harry went on, "it's the compassionate thing to do since she was trying her best."

Here, Bob stood up and objected. "But Donna can really do some stupid things—you have no idea." Bob began pacing around the porch.

"I do have some idea, son," said Harry, nodding his head. "We all do stupid things from time to time. But it's like Rocky striking out with bases loaded. Was his intention to strike out? No, of course not. He wanted to get a hit, to drive in runs, to be a hero. But sometimes things don't work out, despite our good intentions."

"I see your point," said Bob, who had circled

around behind his father and was resting his hands on the back of Harry's chair. "Results and intentions don't always jibe."

"Hey," Harry chuckled. "That was a pretty good listening check. Here's an example," he continued. "One time, as a birthday surprise, Molly had my black Chrysler 300 painted navy blue. She thought the original color looked too much like a hearse. When I saw it, I nearly choked. It was ugly, and, as you can imagine, I was not too gracious about it, even though her intention had been absolutely loving."

"I remember that," Bob said. "You made Mom put it back the way it was." He came back to his place and sat down. "Not a joyous occasion as I recall."

"In those days, I thought the color of my car was a bigger deal than my wife's loving intentions. Silly me."

"Well, I find it much easier to look for loving intentions with Rocky on the ball field than with Donna," Bob admitted, running his hand repeatedly through his wavy hair. "Rocky I can see is trying his best, it's right before my eyes. He swings with all his might. He wants his team to win. But," Bob sighed, adjusting himself in the chair, "when Donna pushes San Antonio in my face, what kind of loving intentions could she have?"

"I don't know," said Harry, "but let's spend a minute and take a shot at finding one or two of them."

The two men sat quietly for a few moments. The older man was the first to speak.

"Come on, Bob" he encouraged. "You should be able to find some positive intention in Donna's behavior."

"Yeah, she's trying to torture me, punish me,

and get revenge," he said, scratching his head.

"Get into her head, son," Harry said gently. "Imagine that she has positive reasons for saying what she says. What could they be?"

Throwing up his hands, Bob said, "I need some help here, Dad."

"Okay." Harry suggested a few tentative possibilities. "Could she be wanting to save your marriage? Could she be trying to be the best wife she knows how to be? Could she be worried about how Rocky is taking this situation? Could she be trying to get through to you in the only way she knows how? Could there be a lot of fearfulness behind her apparent anger, and she's trying to hide it?"

Bob thought for a moment, leaned over, put his elbows on his knees and cradled his face in his hands. "I guess it could be any of those—or none of them. I just don't know."

"That's just the point of this unspoken request. It says to *look for* my loving intentions. Those loving intentions might not be right there in front of your eyes. You've got to look for them."

"So far," admitted Bob, "I have been looking for her bad intentions, counting the reasons why she hates me, collecting the evidence so I can accuse her of wanting to destroy our marriage."

"So, turn your thinking around," said his father. "How would you respond to Donna—no matter how angry and accusatory she might sound—if you knew her intention was to save your marriage?"

"I guess I could more easily swallow some of her cutting remarks."

"Then," Harry continued, "what if she said to

you something like, 'I really want to be the best wife I can be, but nothing like this has ever happened to us before, and I'm responding to you the only way I know how'?"

Bob considered the question for a moment, and began slowly, "I guess I'd say something like, 'Me too. I really want to be the best husband I can be, but nothing like this has ever happened to me before either, and I've been responding to you the only way I know how. But, since we both want to be the best for each other, maybe we can both find another way to communicate that is not so mutually destructive.'"

"I think you've got it, son," encouraged Harry.

"But that's not the way I usually talk."

"That's not the way I used to talk to your mother before my heart attack either, but I had to learn another way of relating—from the heart—and, I'm afraid, so do you. At college, you may be able to teach from the intellect, but in marriage a sharp mind is not enough. Marriage has to be lived from the heart."

CHAPTER 11

The Fifth Unspoken Request

"Well, go on, Dad. Explain the last one."

"Okay. The fifth request is: TELL ME THE TRUTH WITH COMPASSION. If Donna has an issue with you, she can do three things with it. First, she can keep it to herself and stew over it and resent you. Second, she can bad-rap you to her friends. Or, third, she can come talk to you about it. Which of the three would you prefer?"

"Well, clearly the third. The other two are pretty grim."

"Right. And it's ditto for her. If you have an issue with her, she'd prefer the third alternative, too."

Bob got up and started pacing. "I don't know Dad. Lately I've been walking on tiptoe with Donna. Since San Antonio, I've been trying to be Mr. Nice and avoiding confrontations. I'm trying to get out of her doghouse, and she just keeps on punishing me. How long am I going to have to stay in this marital Purgatory?"

"She may have to release a little steam on that unfortunate event, and you may have to sit still for it, but meanwhile, you have a right to voice your concerns as well, not in a punitive way and not as a tit-for-tat counterpunch but as someone who wants to help make things better."

"I'm beginning to see why a person needs to practice all five of these marriage-from-the-heart secrets, not just one or two of them," said Bob. "How could Donna know I'm trying to tell her the truth with compassion, if I don't hear and understand her, if I don't stop making her wrong, if I don't acknowledge her greatness, or if I don't bother to look for her loving intentions?"

"That's it exactly, son," said Harry smiling. "Those five unspoken requests form an integrated system for lovingly managing your marriage—or any other special relationship."

"But there's one thing that bothers me, Dad," Bob broke in. "What happens if I practice honoring those five unspoken requests with Donna, and she doesn't reciprocate, in other words, if she still keeps badgering me?"

"Not to worry, Bob," reassured his father. "With Donna as furious—or frightened—as she may be today, you may have to practice the five secrets consistently for maybe two weeks, maybe more, maybe less. That woman's heart has got to melt. And it will. It's pretty hard for anyone to keep on the attack when the other person shows understanding of your perspective, doesn't attack back, doesn't try to rebut you, is frequently acknowledging your greatness, and affirming your loving intentions. I'll bet that within a week she'll put her sword down, and you'll be able to talk as a loving and concerned couple."

Bob got up to leave. "I've got to go, Dad. I've got a faculty meeting in less than an hour. Thanks for the HEART card." Bob held the card in his hand, so his father could see it. "You've been a champ. A guy couldn't ask for a better father. I'll let you know how things turn out."

"Use that card to do a HEART Check on your progress," his father reminded him, standing up to shake hands. Ram jumped off Harry's lap and ran to the screen door, tail wagging. "Start practicing the five secrets with some of your fellow professors. Start with an easier experiment, I always say. Donna's going to be your big exam."

"I'm sure she will be," admitted Bob. "And I sure need practice. He stopped and stood at the door silently for a minute thinking about the impact of all that his father had just shared. "It's amazing Dad. Amazing that you got the system. More amazing that you were able to do it." Bob had his hand on the doorknob as he looked back. "I wonder if I can."

"Son, my nickname at the refinery was the Abominable No Man. If I could do it, anyone can."

Bob let go of the doorknob and came back to stand in front of his father. "And you think my doing this will actually help Donna get over San Antonio and finally forgive me?"

"Look son," said Harry, putting his hands on his son's shoulders, "there are no guarantees in life, and you have to decide if it's worth it. I'm not unbiased here. I love your family. Donna's like a daughter to us, as well as Mom's business partner. And Rocky's a treasure. I don't want anything to happen to hurt him. So, do I want you to do whatever it takes to save your marriage? You bet I do. But it's your life." Harry looked directly into his son's eyes, "And I'll always be your Dad, no matter what happens."

Bob leaned over and gave his dad a hug. "I know that, Dad. Thanks for sharing the HEART secrets and for the pep talk. I'm going to do my best to keep our little family together."

CHAPTER 12

Molly

Harry was in the kitchen chopping vegetables for a wok recipe he was preparing. Since his retirement three years ago, he had become a decent, if not imaginative, cook specializing in the low-fat dishes required by his post heart attack regimen. He was surprised to discover he enjoyed cooking, noting that vegetables did not complain if they were not sliced perfectly. Molly was even more surprised to see her formerly workaholic husband humming happily in the kitchen these days.

Harry could hear Molly's car pulling into the garage, so he ceased his chopping and poured two Dubonnet cocktails. When Molly came in loaded down with grocery bags, a tail-wagging Ram ran eagerly around her feet.

Harry greeted her at the door, relieved her of

the bags and set them on the counter. "Hi dear," he said, giving her a kiss of welcome.

"Hi, love," she replied, following him into the kitchen. She spied the filled wineglasses. "Oh, thanks. You read my mind," she said taking one of them. "Here's to a beautiful day," she added raising her glass in a toast.

Harry joined her as they clinked glasses. Molly looked a good deal younger than her 65 years. Tall, about five-foot-seven, with a solid, substantial build and brown hair streaked with gray pulled back in a bun, she gave off a feeling of vigor and radiant good health. She had that crinkly look around her eyes of someone who smiled a great deal throughout her years, and her eyes were full of fun. Not for the first time, Harry thought to himself, "How in the world did I ever get so lucky?"

"Did you make an appearance at the office?" Harry inquired, as they sipped their cocktails. Molly had gradually transferred the management responsibility for Hartwell Realty to Donna but still came in once or twice a week to visit with the staff and check everything out.

"I did indeed. The real estate business is booming right along." Molly was taking items out of the grocery bag and handing them to Harry, who in turn put them in the cupboard or the refrigerator. Molly said, "I saw Donna only briefly, but she seemed distracted and in a funk. Definitely not her effervescent self."

Harry shook his head sadly. "I'm afraid there's trouble in Paradise."

"What do you mean?" she asked, anxiety creeping into her voice.

"Bob left here a little while ago, and it seems he

and Donna have hit a rough patch, which could account for Donna's funk. It also seems that our boy might have wandered off the reservation at the recent conference. He's definitely in the soup, and I'm afraid the marriage might be wobbling under the strain." He filled her in on the details.

Molly got up and walked to the window. "That's just awful, Harry. I'd be devastated if anything happened. Is there anything we can do to help?"

Harry also got up and followed her. "Well, I told Bob about what I was like as a husband before the heart attack and what I had done to change, but first, I'm not sure he got it; second, even if he got it, I'm not sure he can implement it; and third, even if he implements it, if Donna is rebuffing his efforts, I'm not sure it'll make any difference."

Molly frowned. "When you say you told him how you changed, how specific were you? Did you tell him about the unspoken requests and everything?"

"Yup, I gave him the full Monte. And he left with a HEART card in his shirt pocket. But their situation is much different than ours was. You were receptive to the changes, delighted even, and your positive reaction encouraged me to keep on trying. According to Bob, Donna's so angry at him, I'm afraid she'll just take his efforts as new opportunities to skewer him for his sins. I'm really worried."

Molly was silent for a while and appeared deep in thought. Harry knew not to interrupt her ruminations and that Molly would report the results when she was ready. In a few minutes, Molly was ready. She looked up as if a light bulb had gone off in her head.

"I have an idea," she said. "There are advantages

to being Donna's professional mentor. One of them is that she is used to listening to me and learning from my experience. We mostly don't talk much about personal stuff. I guess it's hard to have your mother-in-law as a confidante. But I'm wondering if I couldn't make an exception and cross the line this one time."

Harry was intrigued. "What would you say to her, if you crossed the line, as you put it?"

"Well, as you know, it takes two to build a solid marriage. While you were struggling to master the five HEART secrets, I was already practicing most of them. I'm thinking of working the other side of the street, of tipping Donna off about what she could do to re-build their relationship, if that's what she wants."

"That's the key question. If that's what she wants," Harry added.

"I can't imagine that Donna would want to break up their family and blow up Rocky's world. She's probably feeling terribly hurt right now, but I'm hoping there's enough good will left for her to make the effort."

Harry walked over to Molly and gave her a hug. "God bless you, dear. If you can get Donna just to be open, that would be wonderful."

CHAPTER 13

The Arrangement

By the time Donna got out of bed, Rocky had left for school and Bob was off to work. That was part of their arrangement. Early-riser Bob handled the mornings, getting Rocky out of bed, fed breakfast, and out the door on time. Donna was a slow starter, definitely not a morning person. People who woke up energized and cheerful totally mystified her.

The thing that got her going each morning was her five-mile run. She took a regular run around the lake in the municipal park. And, although some mornings she had to force herself to do it, once she started running, she enjoyed it thoroughly and invariably felt good afterward.

Today, as she finished her run and stepped back into the house, she felt a cloudy gray heaviness in her mood. In her head, like a beating tom-tom, she kept hearing over and over a question she couldn't answer: "Why couldn't Bob have kept his side of the bargain?"

Donna felt that she and Bob has tacitly agreed that in this stage of their life, the two top priorities had to be building their respective careers and parenting their precious Rocky. Both careers were highly demanding: Donna's, because selling homes was such a competitive business that it required providing extra service, total availability, and a personal touch in developing relationships with clients and prospective clients. And she also didn't want to disappoint Molly, who had entrusted her with the business that she, Molly, had built over a twenty-year period. Bob had to understand that evenings and weekends were prime "show" time, and if that meant he had to adjust and be on-duty with Rocky, well, that's just the way it was. Welcome to life in the real estate business.

Bob's career had its own set of demands: classes every morning and some afternoons with heavy preparation required for each, meeting with students, grading papers and exams, doing research into arcane topics, and writing articles in journals that had to pass muster with a jury of his peers. Plus helping to coach the varsity soccer team. And all of this work would eventually be evaluated and judged in the decision to grant or withhold tenure, the North Star of an academic career, the ticket to professional success and freedom.

Under their cooperative arrangement, Donna would work at the agency while Rocky was in school but was always there when Rocky got home. She would take him to any medical or dental appointments or any lessons. Most important, Donna took him to baseball practice and got to watch him doing what he loved most.

Bob would return from the University late in the afternoon. Unless, of course, Rocky had a game, in which case Bob would find a way to be there when it started. If Donna did not have appointments over the dinner hour, they would enjoy a rare dinner together, but frequently, like last night, Donna was out showing homes until late. Bob would help Rocky with any homework, play catch in the back yard, and put him to bed.

The arrangement seemed to work, especially for Rocky, who got plenty of special one-on-one time with each parent. But, Donna reflected, it didn't leave much time for Bob and Donna to be together as a couple, to enjoy each other's company and do things together.

Implicit in the arrangement was the clear expectation that neither their demanding careers nor their limited time together nor anything else, for that matter, would erode their commitment to be faithful to each other. Donna had thought Bob was fully on board with their arrangement, but apparently not. She had been shocked and deeply hurt to hear Bob's halting, embarrassed recital of his recent San Antonio conference. And then she turned angry as a hornet. She remembered her stinging words to him that evening. "If you're so unhappy with our arrangement, why haven't you said anything? Why would you go through the motions of your life with me, when all the while you were dissatisfied and frustrated? Why did it finally have to come out sideways, violating my trust by acting out with another woman? Why didn't you just talk to me months ago?"

Angrily, she shook her head involuntarily, as she climbed the stairs to their bedroom and the shower.

"I'll never understand men, at least not my man." Startled at her own words, she wondered, "Is he really still my man? What happens at the next conference? What else may be happening now?"

In spite of herself, Donna began to sob. She didn't know where their relationship—their love and commitment—had gone off the rails or how to get it back on track or, even, whether there was a way back.

CHAPTER 14

Flowers

If it was possible to be both a cynic and a romantic, curly-haired Marvin fit the bill. Professionally, he had to be a cynic. Anyone who studies American politics has to be cynical or be taken for a fool. Marvin, whose penetrating eyes never left you when he talked to you, was nobody's fool. He believed politicians come sincerely, more or less, to believe in the economic interests of their constituents and that Presidents frequently discover international crises occurring just prior to elections. "Wag the Dog" was his favorite movie. Marvin believed that to understand American politics at its core, cynicism was the pre-requisite operating assumption.

But in his personal life Marvin was an unreconstructed romantic. His sharp professional look turned into big brown eyes that were soft, warm and irresistible. When he proposed to Sue, he had rowed her out to a deserted island and gotten down on his knees, engagement ring in pocket, and asked for her hand in marriage. How could she refuse? And of course, she hadn't.

Marvin was worried about his buddy Bob. Bob was in marital doo-doo, largely of his own making. Definitely a dumb move. But, as far as Marvin was concerned, his friend was now acting like a victim, passively absorbing all the slings and arrows that Donna was hurling in his direction. Even when Bob was with Marvin, he was usually slouching around looking like the walking wounded, whining and whimpering about how badly he was being treated. "Poor baby!" Marvin thought to himself. "Shoulda' kept your hands off the 'moichendise,' as my father used to say, or at least you shoulda kept your mouth shut about it." Marvin shook his head in disbelief that his friend would, number one, do such a dumb thing and, number two, act like such a helpless wimp.

In these situations, Marvin believed, the greatest sin was passivity, letting things happen instead of making things happen. Suddenly, he had an inspired idea, the perfect way of helping his downtrodden buddy in an hour of need. He looked up the phone number of Zenith Florist and ordered a dozen red roses sent to Donna with a note signed, "Love from your one and only." Pleased as punch with his inspired act of friendship, he went searching for Bob to tell him. He didn't want Bob looking surprised when Donna thanked him profusely.

He found Bob in a semi-fetal position at his desk staring out the window. "Hey, sport," he said cheerfully as he entered. Then, noting Bob's depressed posture, he added, "Are we moping? Rise up. Your good buddy Marvin has found a way for you to receive redemption. Your non-crime will be forgiven."

Bob gazed up at Marvin as if he were a visitor from another planet. "Oh, and are you a magician now? Have you added the black art of conjuring to your vast array of skills?"

Marvin smiled and spread his long arms in a lordly gesture. "Even better. I decided you needed to stop groveling and try a little tenderness, so I had you send a dozen red roses to your bride with a pithy note."

"You did what?" Bob's rapt attention had crossed over to alarm.

"I sent flowers to your wife—from you."

"Oh terrific, now I'm really cooked. You can stick a fork in me—I'm done."

"No, you're not done. *Au contraire, mon ami,* Donna will love the flowers. Her too, too solid heart will melt. Your time in the guest room will be over—history."

"And pray tell, what did the so-called 'pithy note' say?"

"Just the usual sweet nothings."

Bob was upset. Regardless of whether sending flowers to Donna was a good idea or a bad idea, Marvin had clearly overstepped the boundaries of friendship by doing it for him without checking.

He was just about to give Marvin a piece of his mind, but then he clicked on his conversation with Harry about the five unspoken requests. "What was the one about intentions?" he thought to himself. "Oh yeah, REMEMBER TO LOOK FOR MY LOVING

INTENTIONS. Well heck, what could Marvin's intentions have been here? He clearly wasn't trying to get me in more trouble. In fact, it's obvious he was trying to help me out of an awful situation." So, Bob decided to try out one of his dad's suggestions, to use Marvin's rose-sending situation as a sort of guinea pig for Harry's HEART secrets.

Instead of lambasting Marvin for usurping Bob's autonomy, Bob got up, put his hand on Marvin's shoulder and looked at him straight in the eye. "You know, I could be pissed that you did this all on your own, but I can see that your loving intention was to help me out of a jam. Marvin, you are really a terrific friend."

Marvin looked pleasantly surprised. "Well thanks, buddy. Sometimes my inspirations are not fully appreciated, so I'm glad you caught the drift."

Bob folded his arms pensively. "I still have to figure out whether this is the right time to do flowers."

"You can probably still cancel the order, but I'll tell you," Marvin responded, "with women, it's always the right time to do flowers. They never resent it. There's no such thing as screwing up with flowers. They carry magical properties, a universal solvent to the hardest of feminine hearts."

Bob laughed at his friend's tendency to talk like the famous Greek Oracle at Delphi. "Well, maybe I'll give it a try. Unfortunately, I don't think I have too much to lose."

Marvin returned to his office a few minutes later, and Bob was left pondering two things: the likely impact of the imminent flower delivery and the results of his experiment in honoring what Harry had referred to as an unspoken request. He decided he was dubious about the first but satisfied with the second. Acknowledging Marvin's loving intention had brought them closer and created a nice moment and a warm connection. Blowing up at him would have pushed Marvin away and created distance.

As Bob continued to reflect on the conversation, he realized that more than just one of the HEART secrets had been in play. He took the HEART card out of his shirt pocket and said to himself, "I'll try doing a HEART Check the way Dad does." He began to review each of them and to estimate to what extent he had honored each of the five unspoken requests.

"Let's see," he thought, "First, HEAR AND UNDERSTAND ME: Well, I think Marvin felt reasonably heard and understood, but I didn't really summarize or do listening checks. Second, EVEN IF YOU DISAGREE, PLEASE DON'T MAKE ME WRONG: Hmm, after my shocked initial reaction and a bit of sarcasm, I didn't really attack him. It could have been a lot worse, but I could have been a tad calmer, I guess. Third, ACKNOWLEDGE THE GREATNESS WITHIN ME: I did okay here. I told Marvin I thought he was a terrific friend. Maybe I could have said something about his creativity or his deep insight into feminine psychology. No, that might be stretching it. Fourth, REMEMBER TO LOOK FOR MY LOVING INTENTIONS: Now, that one I really nailed. Fifth, TELL ME THE TRUTH WITH COMPASSION: This one didn't come into play. I wasn't confronting him with more than my reaction."

Bob concluded that, by and large, his experiment in using the HEART secrets had been successful.

Honoring Marvin's unspoken requests, to the extent that he had done so, had served him well. Maybe now he would take the much larger risk of trying them with Donna.

CHAPTER 15

Hesitation

Sue Rogers had a dilemma. As she was driving to work, she was thinking about her friend Donna and had some ideas but didn't know quite how to broach them. Waiting at a red traffic light, she asked herself, "How do you talk to someone about her marriage without being invited? Even when it's as close a friend as Donna?"

Along with raising two young daughters, Sue worked part-time as a counselor in a family planning clinic, and she understood the issue of boundaries. Her clients walked in the door and asked for help, which allowed Sue to bring all her experience and skills to bear on the client's situation. But in the absence of any request for help, a person's marriage was very much his or her own business, and others did not have the right to intrude. In their brief post-tennis match conversation, Donna had shared her pain, and Sue had listened and commiserated but had not sensed any invitation or opening to pursue the matter further.

The light changed to green, but even as Sue moved her car with the flow of traffic, her mind churned on her original question.

Sue was convinced that Donna was focused on the wrong problem. Bob's behavior at the San Antonio conference had been a foolish and thoughtless mistake, but in no way a cause for contemplating divorce. In Sue's view, that event had merely brought to the surface the more serious underlying problems in the marriage, chief of which was that Bob and Donna, aside from co-habiting and co-parenting, didn't seem to have much of a life together. Both were such committed workaholics that very little time was left over for their marriage. "A marriage that is not nourished," thought Sue, "eventually shrivels up and dies." Bob's San Antonio antics, viewed in that light, were the act of a desperate and lonely man, putting up a red warning signal and, perhaps, a cry for help.

Another traffic light turned red and allowed her a moment of personal reverie that took her back to her college days.

Growing up, Sue, like many attractive girls, had been encouraged to trade on her good looks and to hide her brains. In college everyone knew her as a cheerleader; few knew she was a Dean's list psychology honors student. One benefit of her cheerleading role had been the growing intensity of her cheering for a certain curly-haired forward on the basketball team. That's how she had met and fallen in love with Marvin.

As she pulled into a parking space at the clinic, Sue turned the dilemma over and over in her mind: "If a friend were about to walk into an open manhole," she asked herself, "wouldn't I warn her or help her avoid it? So what am I afraid of?"

"Well, for starters," she thought, as she locked her car door, "I'm afraid that Donna would tell me to mind my own business. And my unasked for help would push her away and injure our friendship." She was also afraid Donna would see her perspective as taking Bob's side, as defending Bob's behavior as no big deal. Hadn't Donna already referred to Marvin as an idiot for expressing a similar view? Sue remembered one of her professors cautioning the class that "all help is not helpful."

"To help or not to help, that is the question," Sue thought, paraphrasing Shakespeare, as she opened the clinic door. Her last thought as she entered the crowded waiting room was: "Or perhaps what I must do, jumping nimbly from *Hamlet* to *MacBeth,* is screw my courage to the sticking point."

Her first client was waiting and eager to be seen, so thoughts of Donna and Bob were put on the back burner.

Meantime, Molly sat at home in her kitchen with her second cup of coffee, having similar ruminations. "How can a mother-in-law offer advice to her daughter-in-law," she wondered, "without being suspected of a fatal bias? Won't Donna just see me as defending my poor misunderstood son? Have we built up enough mutual trust in all our years as business partners, as well as in-laws, for me to offer help in saving and re-building her marriage? This is a tough one," she thought. After sounding so confident in her conversation with Harry, now she was worried about making things worse than they already were.

CHAPTER 16

The Game

Rocky stood on the pitcher's mound, leaning in towards home plate to get the signal from his catcher Matt Sanchez. The batter was Wally Rigby, first baseman and clean-up hitter for the Stingers. Rocky's team, the Rottweilers, was leading 3–2, but the Stingers had the tying run on first in the final inning with two outs and their best hitter up to bat.

Bob sat in the last row of the bleachers, silently hoping that Rocky would find a way to get the batter out. The Stingers were defending champions of the Little League and were in first place this year. This was the make-up game for the rainout. After striking out the first batter in the inning and getting the second on a weak tap to shortstop, Rocky had issued a rare walk to the third batter allowing the dangerous Rigby to come to bat.

Bob had spent hours and years teaching Rocky how to pitch. Ten-year-olds were too young to pitch a curve ball without risking injury, but Bob had shown Rocky how to throw accurately inside and outside, high and low, and how to change speeds, all of which was designed to put the batter off balance.

Rigby was a big, burly kid with the confident look of someone who was used to doing well in sports. It was hard to believe he was just eleven-years-old.

Matt signaled for a fastball and placed his big catcher's mitt slightly to his left, close to the right-handed batter. Rocky pitched from a stretch, checked the runner at first, and fired. "Ball one," the umpire croaked. The pitch just missed inside.

Bob groaned. The pitch had been close. Donna sat a few feet away on the bench, trying to look interested in the proceedings. The drama of the moment eluded her.

The second pitch was low. Ball two. The third pitch was right over, and Rigby took it. Strike one. The count was now 2–1. Matt called for a change-up, the slowest pitch, and put his mitt right, on the outside corner. Rigby swung hard and connected, but was early and fouled it off to deep left. Two and two.

Now Matt came out to the mound to talk to Rocky. "You want to waste one, see if he bites?"

Rocky pondered this and then answered, "Naw, let's get him right here."

"Okay," said Matt, "your heat, man—keep it low."

Bob clenched his fists. He knew Rocky didn't like to throw waste pitches, so this was it, the moment of truth. Rocky went into his stretch and threw it with all the force his ten-year-old body could muster. Rigby swung and the ball made a loud, resounding thwack as it left the bat and headed for deep left center. The left fielder hesitated for a moment, then belatedly turned around and started running back. The ball landed beyond his outstretched glove and kept rolling. Meanwhile, the runner on first scored, and Rigby was steaming around third. The left fielder retrieved the ball, threw it to the shortstop who whirled and fired it to the catcher, but Rigby had already slid safely into home for a homerun. The game was over. The Stingers had won 4–3.

The other Stingers surrounded Rigby cheering and patting him on the back.

Rocky slumped on the mound. The pitch had been right over the center of the plate, a fat pitch, and Rigby had clobbered it. He had lost the game for the team. He felt awful. As he walked toward the sidelines, he was fighting back tears.

Donna didn't know what to say. She put her hands on his shoulders and looked directly at him. He looked away. With motherly love, she wanted to console him, so she said, "It's okay, Rocks, you'll get them next time."

Rocky turned back and glared at her. "No, I won't, he just creamed my best pitch." Disgusted with himself, he spat out, "I really suck."

Bob came over and gave Rocky a hug. "Take a walk with me, son." They walked together arm in arm away from the field. Rocky lost it.

"Dad, I really blew it. I let everyone down," he sobbed.

"I know you feel bad, but tell me something. Did you do your best today? Did you give it everything you had?"

Rocky answered through his tears, "I did, Dad, I really did."

As men typically do when caught up in strong emotion, father and son didn't turn to each other but walked side by side, looking straight ahead.

"Well, son, if you did your best, and I believe you did, that's all you can do in life. There are no guarantees of victory. No team wins every game, no batter bats 1000, and no pitcher throws shutouts every time out. All you can ever do is your best. And you did it. So I'm proud of you, regardless of how it turned out. I think you're a darn good pitcher and you have the heart of a lion. Today the lion got nicked. Tomorrow he might prevail. But a lion is always a lion."

Rocky smiled through his tears. "Yeah, Dad, I know. Next time, I'm going to hang that Wally Rigby out to dry." As they walked over together to where Donna was standing, Rocky said, "Hey, Mom, you're right, I'll get him next time."

Donna gave Rocky a big hug, which he now welcomed, and she gave Bob a perplexed look.

CHAPTER 17

Instant Replay

After Rocky was in bed, Bob sat down on the living room couch. Now he had the chance to think about Rocky's anguished reaction to losing the game and about his own response to his son's pain.

He remembered his dad's five unspoken requests, and though he hadn't planned it or consciously tried to respond to the five requests, he decided to review the post-game conversation with Rocky to see to what extent he might have inadvertently honored any of the five. He took out the card his father had given him and did a HEART Check.

"On the first one, HEAR AND UNDERSTAND ME," Bob thought to himself "I did one thing right, namely, acknowledge my son's feelings. I said: 'I know you feel bad,' validating that I heard and understood what Rocky was going through. Maybe hearing the feeling was as important or even more important than hearing the words.

"The second one, EVEN IF YOU DISAGREE, PLEASE DON'T MAKE ME WRONG, didn't apply here. There was no disagreement, but I certainly didn't come anywhere near blaming him for the defeat.

"On the third one, ACKNOWLEDGE THE GREATNESS WITHIN ME, I did really well. I told Rocky I was proud of him, that I knew he had done his best, and that he had the heart of a lion. Like Rigby, I hit a homerun on this one.

"On the fourth one, REMEMBER TO LOOK FOR MY LOVING INTENTIONS, I did all right here too. I told Rocky I knew he had done his best.

"On the fifth one, TELL ME THE TRUTH WITH COMPASSION, I told him the truth that life holds no guarantees, that no one is perfect, and that there will be other days and other games, but I said nothing in a confrontational mode. It wouldn't have been appropriate."

As Bob continued pondering his post-game conversation with his emotionally distraught son and measuring it against the five HEART secrets, he concluded that first, he had done pretty well with no advance preparation or planning. Second, Rocky had emerged from the conversation feeling unburdened and much better. And third, the conversation had been a significant shared moment that had brought them closer to each other.

Bob was beginning to glimpse the power of the HEART secrets and to sense their potential for healing.

CHAPTER 18

Feedback

Normally, the weekly meetings of Unfaithful Anonymous consisted of a series of confessional monologues in which participants stood at the front of the room and talked about their own experiences and their efforts to change. The role of the other participants was to listen sympathetically without judgement and with full acceptance and compassion for the speaker. At the end, they were to applaud, regardless of what the speaker said. The setting was designed to encourage honest self-disclosure and self-reflection.

Once a month, Unfaithful Anonymous altered its format and held a Feedback Meeting. At these monthly events, the participants stood in a circle and, one at a time, each participant would go around the inside of the circle, stopping in front of each other participant and asking: "What do you think I am missing?"

The theory behind this exercise was that all human beings have blind spots and that often others can shed useful light on them. Participants were encouraged to "shoot straight" with their feedback and not hold back out of fear. Recipients of feedback were instructed to thank anyone who offered feedback and to consider it as food for thought, neither accepting it nor rejecting it out of hand.

After the special feedback format was explained, Bob felt a growing uneasiness. He looked around the room at the others seated there. By their facial expressions and nervous body movements, he could tell that no one was really looking forward to this event. He wondered if they expected it to turn into an adversarial thing, where their usual accepting attitudes toward each other are turned upside down.

Since this was only his second meeting, he didn't feel he had enough data to offer any useful feedback to anyone. Certainly nothing negative. And, by the same token, he doubted that he would get any insightful or valuable feedback from people he had barely met. But he was curious enough about the strange process to participate, despite his misgivings. In fact, as the leader asked the group to stand and begin the process, Bob was reviewing the HEART secrets in his mind and wondering whether and how he might employ them tonight.

As the first participant stood in front of him and asked the question, "What do you think I am missing?" Bob responded, "Sorry, I can't think of anything." And with a shrug of his shoulders he added, "I honestly don't know."

When the second participant faced him, thinking

of the HEART principles, he said, "Maybe you don't give yourself enough credit for all your effort." It was no gem of wisdom falling from his lips, but at least it was encouraging. He was aware that he was up next.

When it was his turn to enter the circle, Bob stood smiling before the first group member and duly asked the question, expecting similar demurrals. "What do you think I am missing?" he asked.

The first person, a short balding man, responded: "You're in denial. You're as unfaithful as anyone in here."

Bob felt the emotional arrow pierce him and had to struggle not to offer a rebuttal. Definitely a straight shooter, he thought. Aims right for the heart. Bob's "thanks" to him was almost a whisper.

The second person, a thin-lipped man still in his business suit, said: "You think you have to unzip your fly to be unfaithful. That's crap."

Bob thought, damn right I do. A blood-red anger was rising to his face. He shifted on his feet for a few moments to control himself. All he could do for a "thanks" to this fellow was a slight nod of his head.

The third person, with an almost mocking voice, said: "What if your wife went off to a Realtors Convention and made out with a slick hunk of a realtor—would that be just fine with you?"

The fourth person, soft-spoken and earnest, said: "What you don't get is that being unfaithful is a head and heart thing, not just a sex thing."

The fifth person, a man whom Bob knew had five children, said: "If you're not taking care of your marriage, you're not taking care of your family."

And so it went, around the circle.

The last person, who had heard the comments of all the others and feeling bad for Bob, said: "You seem like an okay guy, but somewhere you got off the path."

Bob was jolted by the repeated salvos of feedback, all rejecting the notion he had floated at the last meeting, that he didn't belong there. Food for thought, indeed.

Could he be right and all of them wrong?

As the rest of the group made their way around the circle to receive their feedback, Bob was so numb—almost in shock—that he had no recollection of what he had said to any of them. In fact, it was only near the end of the meeting that he was able to stop the chaos of thoughts and feelings swirling around inside and be present to the group.

Before they adjourned, one of the older participants reminded the group of something he called the "horse concept." He said, "If someone calls me a horse, I'm going to think he's crazy. If two of you tell me I'm a horse, I might think about it for a moment, but I might conclude the two of you were in cahoots. But if all of you, a whole roomful of people, all tell me I'm a horse, it's possible all of you are wrong—it's POSSIBLE!—but probably, I've got to go out and buy me a saddle. So, as you leave here tonight, I encourage you to reflect on what you heard—each of us got a million dollars worth of feedback—and consider whether you need to buy any saddles."

As Bob turned to leave, he looked down at his feet, half expecting to see hooves.

CHAPTER 19

Insecurities

When Donna returned from her morning run, she noticed that the screen door was ajar. There was something placed behind it. She opened the door and was surprised to see a vase with a dozen red roses sitting there. She read the attached note: "With love from your one and only."

A brief, troubling thought flickered across her mind, "You might be my one and only, but am I yours?"

Donna had grown into an attractive woman but, as a child, she had felt like anything but. Tall for her age as a teenager, towering over all the boys in her class, gawky with braces, she had regarded herself as homely and unlikely to draw any male attention ever.

Time had worked its customary wonders. The braces disappeared, the boys grew up, and her awkwardness grew into a supple athletic grace. Even her height, 5'10, gave her an advantage in soccer in reaching for headers and turning them into goals.

In college she was regarded as a "babe with brains," as well as a star athlete, but even so, she carried with her a grain of insecurity from her ungainly youth. Thrilled when Bob pursued and then proposed to her, she sometimes worried that he might someday discover her limitations and look for somebody better. So, the San Antonio event had a deeper resonance for her than it might have in that it confirmed her worst childhood fears.

As she carried the vase inside, she proceeded to experience a complex mixture of reactions, from suspicion of Bob's motive—was he looking for cheap grace?—to resentment at the blatant manipulation the flowers represented.

As she put the floral arrangement on the hall table just to look at it, a fleeting smile reflected her own susceptibility. For a moment she half-humorously saw herself confronting Bob with the taunt, "Why not diamonds instead of flowers?" But underneath, at a core level, Donna was secretly pleased. However clumsy the gesture, she understood that the flowers signified that Bob cared. And, touching one of the roses, then leaning over to inhale its sweetness, she discovered to her amazement that she cared that Bob cared.

Bob's gesture, thoughtful as it was, didn't change some basic realities. She was still dissatisfied with their separate, parallel lives and still hurt by what she considered Bob's dalliance. But the hard feeling of anger and resentment that had risen up in defense of her hurt had softened just a bit. She looked up to inspect her face in the hall mirror as if to verify that the hurt had indeed softened.

Donna, rubbing her chin and looking around,

pondered where to put the flowers. Not in the living room, that might give the false impression all was forgiven. Not in what used to be their bedroom, that might imply that the gesture had penetrated the walls of her heart like some sort of Trojan horse. Not in the kitchen, that would be too tacky. She decided that the proper spot for the vase and roses was in the guest room that Bob was inhabiting; that Bob should share his space with his gesture and decide what it meant for him.

Satisfied with her decision, she picked up the vase, walked purposefully with it into the guestroom, and placed it on the dresser.

CHAPTER 20

Listening

When Bob opened the front door, he could tell that Donna was in the kitchen. Rocky, he supposed, was upstairs either doing his homework or pouring over the batting averages listed in the latest edition of Sports Illustrated. Bob could guess which. He walked into the brightly lit kitchen.

With antennae tuned for Donna's feeling tone, he greeted her with a neutral "Hi dear."

Donna responded lightly with, "Hi. Thanks for the roses. They're lovely."

Bob, deciding the emotional temperature had indeed warmed a few degrees, silently thanked Marvin for both the idea and its implementation. "I'm going to change. I want to check in with Rocky and I'll be back in a few minutes," he said as he turned in the direction of the guest bedroom.

On his way, he noticed the flowers were not on the hall table nor, when he peered in, were they in the living room. "Perhaps she put them in the master bedroom," he mused. That would be nice.

He was puzzled when he found the vase of roses in the guest bedroom—his room—but was relieved that at least Donna hadn't thrown it at him, as he had imagined in his catastrophic fantasy. As he removed his sport coat and tie, he decided that the flowers' location was Donna's way of saying, "Okay, just because you did something nice, don't assume you're entirely out of the doghouse." He could live with that, he thought, as he washed up and changed into casual clothes.

All day long, Bob had pondered the feedback he had received from the other Unfaithful Anonymous participants. His initial instinct to discount it had been overwhelmed by its near unanimity, namely, that his technical, neo-Clintonian defense that he hadn't committed the act of infidelity was irrelevant. As a result, he was eager for an opportunity to re-open the conversation with Donna that she had terminated so abruptly two days ago. Also, armed with his father's five HEART secrets, he wanted to see if doing a better job of listening might make a difference.

Bob walked across the hall and greeted Rocky, who indeed was buried in *Sports Illustrated*. "Dinner's almost ready," he said to his son.

They chatted for a few moments, and after getting Rocky to agree to shift his attention to school work after dinner, Bob turned to leave. "How I love you, kiddo!" he said silently as he closed Rocky's bedroom door.

When he came back down, Donna was still

there, setting the table. "Don't you have an appointment tonight?" he asked.

"I re-scheduled it. I was hoping we could have some time to talk while Rocky was doing his homework."

"Great. I appreciate that." Bob was reminded of the story of a sailboat with two people in it, each leaning out over an opposite side of the boat. As one leaned out further, the other had to reciprocate to keep the boat on an even keel. The risk of moving towards the center of the boat was that the other person would not reciprocate, and the boat would capsize. Bob realized that something significant had just happened: Donna had taken in the gift of flowers as Bob moving toward the center of their marital boat and had just reciprocated by postponing an appointment to show a house, an act that could easily cost her a sale and a commission. Bob knew well that, for Donna, staying home tonight was a big deal and a huge sacrifice. She had made a move toward the center of the boat.

After dinner, Rocky departed with his father's words, "No *Sports Illustrated* until your homework's done," bringing a rueful smile. "That was our deal."

"Okay, Dad, but the Mets had a really great week."

After he did dishes, Bob asked Donna, "Would now be a good time for you to explain the marital boycott treatment?"

They went into the living room and sat down in separate easy chairs facing each other.

"I appreciated the flowers," Donna began, "but I don't want to be bought off by them. I was absolutely shocked and hurt to hear your casual, breezy account of what happened at your San Antonio conference, of your groping in public with that woman. I felt discounted, disrespected, and humiliated. And I can imagine your Wellington history colleagues sharing the juicy tidbit with their spouses and friends."

Bob desperately wanted to reassure her that there were no colleagues present, but he was focusing hard on the first unspoken request, HEAR AND UNDERSTAND ME, and was determined to honor it.

"So, Donna, you were both surprised and hurt that I would carry on in public with another woman. You felt disrespected and were concerned that you would be the butt of gossip here in the community."

"Right," she continued, "and I was angry as hell that you would violate our marriage in that way. If you're unhappy, why couldn't you just talk to me instead of acting it out with another woman? It felt like such a betrayal."

Her voice had risen, and she paused to listen for any movement upstairs from Rocky, but heard none.

Bob responded, "So you were, and presumably still are, angry at me for acting out instead of talking to you, and the acting out feels like a betrayal of your trust in me." It just killed Bob to hear this and to have to repeat it. In his mind, he would do anything not to injure Donna's trust in him. But there it was, and there was no escaping it.

Donna nodded. "You got it. So, now you understand why I insisted you go to Unfaithful Anonymous. You can be an unfaithful jerk without having sex. By the way, I am glad you didn't have sex with her, because if you had, I can tell you, you wouldn't even rate the guestroom. You'd be out of here."

"You're glad I didn't commit the act of adultery, because it would be a deal-buster for you on our marriage." Maybe, Bob thought to himself, not half as glad as I am.

"Yeah, I think so," said Donna, nodding her head a number of times. "I know infidelity is accepted in some cultures and it's certainly rampant in ours, but I don't want to live that way." She paused for a moment. "And I didn't think you did either."

Bob decided that having listened relentlessly to all of Donna's feelings and provided the evidence of his listening with listening checks, this might be an opportunity to respond.

"Donna, of course I don't want to live that way. I love you and want to stay married to you, and be in a faithful, monogamous relationship, like we've always had. I made a mistake and I apologize with all my heart. It will never happen again, I assure you. The folks at Unfaithful Anonymous helped me understand the idea of emotional infidelity. I do understand now why you regard my actions as unfaithful. I accept it, and I am so sorry. But I very much want to know what else I have to do to get out of your doghouse and back into your good graces. And sometime, not now, I want to talk about other issues in our marriage."

Tears appeared on Donna's face. "Well, I'm glad to hear you say that. And I don't know what it will take. Maybe just time. I'd like to forgive you and get through it, but I've been shaken, and it will take time."

Bob gave her his handkerchief for her tears. "You'll have all the time you need. I'm not going anywhere."

At that point, Rocky yelled from upstairs, "Dad, can you quiz me on the state capitals? I have a test tomorrow."

Bob shrugged at Donna, got up, planted a kiss on the top of her head, and, smiling, went upstairs to join Rocky.

CHAPTER 21

Reflections

After Bob had finished helping Rocky master the fifty state capitals and get settled into bed, he looked for Donna but she had also gone to bed, so Bob retired to his place of exile, the guest room.

As he lay on his back on top of the bedspread, still dressed and looking up in the dark towards the ceiling, he thought about his conversation earlier in the evening with Donna. How well had he done, he wondered, in honoring her unspoken requests? Time for a HEART Check.

On the first one, HEAR AND UNDERSTAND ME, he knew he had done well. He had been sorely tempted to interrupt, to defend himself, to explain, and even to counterpunch at numerous points, but he had dutifully bitten his tongue. And he had done listening checks, letting Donna know that he was receiving her message accurately, however hard it was to accept. He was surprised his tongue wasn't bleeding from the effort. Fortunately, the unwelcome feedback he had received previously at Unfaithful Anonymous had prepared him for the ordeal.

He was struck by the power of the simple technique of summarizing someone's ideas or feelings. If you argued or offered a rebuttal, it was often like throwing gasoline on a fire: the conflict escalated. But if you were disciplined enough to do listening checks, it was sort of like a bullfighter letting the angry bull go through a cape instead of getting gored. He smiled at the idea of a stadium full of aficionados shouting "Olé!" each time he had done a listening check to one of Donna's points.

And he noticed that, after a while, each time he had done a listening check, her angry tone lost some of its steam. By the end, just as Rocky interrupted them, her feeling tone was almost conversational. So, one of the results of honoring this particular unspoken request was that it had the effect of calming the other person, allowing the angry storm to pass. Another result, he realized, was that by the end Donna was able to hear and understand him. His insight was that listening is reciprocal: a good listener gets listened to. Very interesting, he thought to himself.

"How about the other four unspoken requests?" he asked himself. "Well, on the second one, EVEN IF YOU DISAGREE, PLEASE DON'T MAKE ME WRONG, I did pretty well too. There's a lot I could blame Donna for, but I restrained myself. On the third one, ACKNOWLEDGE THE GREATNESS WITHIN ME, I did zilch. I might have gotten around to it, but

Rocky's homework intruded. Too bad, but I'll have other chances. On the fourth one, REMEMBER TO LOOK FOR MY LOVING INTENTIONS, well, I didn't really get around to that either, even though I know she has them. After all, she cancelled a sales opportunity to have this conversation. On the fifth one, TELL ME THE TRUTH WITH COMPASSION, maybe I scratched the surface by apologizing and announcing that I wanted to talk about other issues, but until I've done it, I haven't really honored this request either. I'd say I batted two-for-five on this HEART Check. A good start, but I've got to do better. Anyway, these unspoken requests are a great road map and a terrific scorecard. They're really helping me put my marriage back together. I just hope it isn't too late."

CHAPTER 22

Careers

After his two morning classes, one on American History in the 20th century, the other on the U.S. Civil War and Reconstruction, Bob generally went to the campus library to continue his research. He was reading microfiche slides of cable traffic between the U.S. Department of State and the U.S. Embassy to Hungary in Budapest in the time before the Hungarian Revolution of 1956, searching for evidence that America had promised military support if the Hungarians revolted. So far, he had not found a "smoking gun."

The thesis appeared promising because of the background. President Eisenhower had campaigned for the Presidency in 1952 with a promise to "roll back the Iron Curtain," an idea that had emanated from his Secretary of State, John Foster Dulles. It sounded good at the time but carried a risk of starting World War III, if the Soviet Union took umbrage at American military units operating in the Soviet sphere close to the borders of the Russian motherland.

In the event, history had played a nasty trick on the Hungarian freedom fighters; their hour of glory was taken over and eclipsed by the Suez Crisis of the same year. Great Britain, France, and Israel, acting in concert, invaded Egypt and reclaimed the Suez Canal that President Nasser had just nationalized. The Soviet Union threatened to intervene. President Eisenhower, sensing the danger of the moment, broke with his allies and, in effect, told them to stand down and return control of the Suez to Egypt.

As these events were playing out in the Middle East, Soviet tanks rolled into Budapest and crushed the Hungarian revolution. The Americans did nothing to prevent this outcome. As the leaders of the revolt, Imre Nagy and Pal Maleter, were sent to the Soviet Union to be executed, many Hungarians believed they had been betrayed by false promises from America, especially by those Radio Free Europe programs that almost seemed to promise the Hungarians American support.

Bob suspected the Hungarians were correct in believing the United States had promised to support them, but Eisenhower and Dulles had denied it. If he could locate an indisputable piece of evidence, the ensuing article would make a big enough splash to ensure that Bob Hartwell would receive tenure at Wellington College. So, every day Bob read another series of boring cables in hopes that today he would discover gold.

During a quiet moment looking out a library window, he wondered if his fascination with the rebellious but unsupported Hungarians had anything to do with his current life.

"Why do I identify with the Hungarians?" he asked himself. "Well," he mused, "they weren't happy with the oppressive regime they were living in. And I'm not too happy with the regime I'm in at home, either. It's pretty oppressive."

He scratched his head and considered another side of the issue. "But the revolutionaries in Hungary were getting run over by tanks, being executed, or sent off to work camps in the frozen tundra. And I'm still alive. On the other hand, for me nights in that guest room feel emotionally colder than Siberia."

Turning back to his microfiche slides, he smiled at another part of the analogy that had just occurred to him. "No wonder I can identify with those Hungarians. Believing in the siren song of Radio Free Europe, their prospects looked very appealing. I found Maritza appealing, too. I guess the grass always looks greener on the other side of the wall," he said to himself, "especially when you're under a tough regime."

And Donna's regime had been tough for a long time. However, he could not deny that he was proud of what she had accomplished professionally.

When Donna had first started working for Hartwell Realty, there were three realtors on staff, all women, including Molly who was not only the owner but also Donna's new mother-in-law. That was thirteen years ago. A lot had changed since then. For one thing, Donna was now a 50% owner of the firm in partnership with Molly. For another, there were now nine realtors, seven women and two men, not including Molly, who was semi-retired and left the active management to Donna. Under Donna's leadership, Hartwell Realty was growing and profitable, having become one of the leading real estate agencies in the county.

Donna was convinced, and she had told Bob so many times, that the key to business success was the personal touch, the relationship created between the agent and the client family, whether sellers or buyers. Based on that conviction, she trained each new hire on relationship skills as well as the technical and legal aspects of the job, so that each agent would reflect and embody the personal touch Donna viewed as their competitive edge. Bob couldn't help admiring Donna's wisdom in that.

But there was a downside to Donna's approach, which he felt more and more as the years went on. Despite her efforts to train the agents and, in effect, replicate herself, she knew that none of the other agents quite had her touch and that they often lost sales that she would have gotten. This was one of the reasons she devoted so much of her time to sales. She mostly took on the largest, most expensive homes on the seller's side and, on the buyer's side, tended to handle personally couples who were looking for those special kinds of homes.

A six-percent commission on a half-million or a million-dollar home added significantly to the bottom line. Bob couldn't argue with that, because she had begun to create a nest egg for them and for Rocky's college education.

"It just kills me to let one of them get away," she had said to him one night at dinner a few years ago. He could even now hear the forcefulness of her assertion, "If you want to do it right, do it yourself!"

So, he mused, in addition to managing the business and supervising the other eight agents, Donna ended up showing as many homes to as many couples as anyone else. In effect, she had doubled her workload.

Bob could not deny that both he and Donna greatly enjoyed their work. He was fascinated with discovering how individual decisions had huge unanticipated impacts in history. Donna loved helping people find and fall in love with the home of their dreams.

"Neither of us resents the demands of our careers," Bob said to an imaginary Donna, "although I do look forward to having my tenure ordeal over and done with."

They both liked using their talents fully, feeling successful, and getting the financial rewards associated with success. If, at that moment, either had been asked how their career was going, both would have responded: "Great!"

"But, if at that moment someone had asked us how our marriage was going," Bob thought, "I'm sure the answer would be quite different."

CHAPTER 23

A Chat

Sue and Donna were enjoying a post-tennis iced tea on Donna's deck. Again, Sue had won the match handily, as she had done the previous week. She was less surprised to have won this time, concluding that marital problems are probably not conducive to playing your best tennis. As they sat quietly, each engrossed in her own thoughts, Sue decided that now was the time for her to broach the subject. She had finally figured out her approach. Between inflicting un-asked-for help and maintaining discrete silence, there was a middle way, namely, offering help but making it an offer that could be refused.

With great trepidation, she began. "Donna, I've been thinking a lot about your and Bob's situation, and I have some thoughts I'd like to share, if you want to hear them. If you don't, I would certainly understand,

and I'd be fine with keeping them to myself."

Donna looked up and forced a smile. "As you can imagine, that's practically all I've been thinking about. Sure. Go ahead. I've been buried in my own thoughts for so long, it would be refreshing to hear someone else's."

Sue gave an audible sigh of relief. "This is going to take a while, so bear with me. As part of my job with the clinic, I have to stay current on the research about marriage and parenting. I'm on the e-mail list of an organization called the Coalition of Marriage, Families and Couples Education, so I get a daily update."

Donna nodded, so Sue continued.

"You know I care a lot about you and Bob and Rocky, so I have a personal stake in this. As your friend, I have two concerns, one about the possibility you might be considering divorce, the other about how you and Bob are managing your time within your marriage." She paused and looked over at Donna. "Are you sure it's okay for me to talk about these things?"

Donna was hesitant but definitely intrigued. "Sue, there is no one else in my life, besides Bob, who I could have this conversation with. Please, go ahead."

Sue took another breath. "Okay, I have to admit I am scared that you and Bob will get a divorce."

Donna nodded again, as if to say, "That's one of the options I'm seriously considering." Sue went on. "And the main part of my fear is the possible adverse impact on Rocky. The research is now showing that children tend to be emotionally healthier and better adjusted when they grow up in stable, nurturing homes with both parents present."

Donna nodded her head sadly. "I worry about

the same thing, even without the research."

Sue continued, "But even if you decide to stay together, which I'm rooting for and praying for with all my heart, I have a second concern." She took another deep breath. This was the point she feared Donna would take as criticism of her life choices and become defensive. "Between your careers and parenting, to an outsider like me it looks like there is no time left over for you and Bob to do anything together. You both like sports, but never do sports together. You both like movies, but never go. You don't take vacations or weekends without Rocky. As far as I can tell, you don't even go out for an evening together, except on rare occasions. I mean, I think it's great you both have careers you feel passionate about. And I think you're both super parents. But how do you build an intimate relationship with no time for just the two of you?"

Donna had started feeling uncomfortable as Sue began describing her and Bob's life together. The description was close enough to accurate, maybe too close. But it disturbed her to hear it anyway.

"Well, you're right," Donna blurted, then sighed, "except I don't see a way out."

Donna seemed ready to talk, so Sue listened.

"I know that something will have to give," she began, "only the problem is there's no slack in the system. Take Bob's situation. Right now, he's up for tenure. He's trying for one more big article before they decide. If he backs off that and it costs him tenure, it will finish him at Wellington. What's he supposed to do? That's Bob's dilemma.

"In my case, I'm running a business that's growing each year, and I'm running it for Molly. I can't afford to do anything less than a maximum effort on Hart-well Realty," she continued as Sue listened. "There's too much good competition out there. And then there's parenting. I appreciate your comment about us being good parents. Thank you. I think we are doing a reasonably good job with Rocky, and that makes it really unthinkable to do less."

Donna had presented her case. Sue remained silent, still listening.

After a moment, Donna leaned over the table, as if to get closer to her friend for a confrontation, "Let me ask you a question, Sue. You and Marvin have two careers. And you have two young daughters. What do you do? Do you and Marvin have any spare time for togetherness?"

Sue took note of Donna's defensive response. She was actually relieved that Donna had asked her a question, which in effect gave her permission to continue and to offer an alternative model—namely, hers and Marvin's.

"Well, Marvin's career pressures are similar to Bob's, minus the tenure problem, which I fully understand. We fortunately passed that hurdle a few years ago, and I'm sure Bob will too, but I know how stressful it is. My career is less time-consuming than yours, but the hours overlap with Marvin's so, before Carol and Annette were both full-time in school, we had to use childcare. Now, I get home just before they do, so mostly, we're covered."

Donna, thirsty from the intensity of their conversation, took a sip of her iced tea.

"Marvin and I have an untouchable date night every Wednesday night. That's our first-line solution for togetherness. We get a babysitter or Marvin's mom. We've only missed once, when Carol had just had an appendectomy. We do different things, a movie, a dinner, a play, a concert — it really doesn't matter. It's time just for us.

"Another thing we do is once every two months we'll take off for a weekend. Go to New York, go backpacking upstate, stay in a motel, go cross-country skiing. Once again, the content or activity doesn't matter. It's about the priority we're giving to our marriage."

Donna was listening intently, so Sue went on.

"Our marriage is our top number one priority. Everything else springs from that source. Our parenting of the girls, our energy for our careers. We take care of it. We make sure our Good Will banks are full. If we need to argue or fight, we do it. As friends and allies. As partners for the duration. Our marriage comes first."

"Your marriage comes first, before your careers, even before parenting?" Donna asked quizzically, as if it were a new idea to her.

"That's right," replied Sue. "It's like on an airplane, you're told to put on your own oxygen mask before your child's. We take care of our marriage so we can, over the long haul, do a good job of parenting. We never forget that, and sometimes, we need to remind each other. That's what we do. It's not always easy or convenient, but it's just what we do."

Donna got up and cleared the iced tea glasses from the table. "That's remarkable," she said. "I've always noticed how easy and warm the two of you were together, but I never understood where it came from. I'm envious of you. Someday, maybe Bob and I will be able to do what you're doing. But I don't see it happening for a while. Quite a while."

Sue let the silence hang in the air. Finally, she said, "Well, thanks for listening. I hope it wasn't too upsetting." She got up to leave.

Donna responded ruefully, "No, it's good to know the road not taken. Thank you, and I'll see you soon."

CHAPTER 24

The Ride Home

The Rottweilers had just defeated the hapless and inaptly named Line Drives by the lopsided score of 8–1. Rocky had pitched well, allowing only four hits and no walks, and had also had gotten two hits and an RBI. Not a bad day's outing. As he got into his mother's car, he was feeling great.

"Boy, we sure creamed them, Mom. They never knew what hit them."

"Yeah, you did, Rocks," she replied. "You were terrific."

Bob waved as he walked past their car on the way to retrieving his own car.

"Mom, how come you're mad at Dad?" he asked as he strapped his seat belt on.

Donna gripped the steering wheel harder. "What makes you think I'm mad at Dad?"

"Well, why does he sleep in the guest room?"

Donna inwardly grimaced, but she replied in an offhand tone. "That's because he snores so loud I couldn't sleep."

"Is he going to be there forever, then? What if we have guests?"

"We'll worry about that when we have guests. What's your homework situation look like tonight?" She hastened to change the subject, hoping Rocky would follow her to the new subject.

"Some reading in geography and a spelling test. No sweat." Rocky said, but refocused on his original subject. "You know, Dad should try wearing one of those Band-Aid things over his nose like football players wear—maybe that would help his snoring."

Donna was extremely uncomfortable with the conversation about Bob's mythical snoring problem. Nevertheless, she said, "Good idea. I'll suggest it to him and I'll be sure to tell him it was your idea."

Rocky sat up in his seat. "Oh, I forgot to tell you. Matt invited me to sleep over Saturday night. The Sanchezes want to take us to the new Adam Sandler movie. I really like him—he's such a weird character. Is that okay?"

Donna realized, since she had no real estate appointments scheduled, that this would leave Bob and her without a buffer. She had mixed feelings about this. "Well, I'll run it by your Dad, but I can't see why not."

As she parked the car and walked into the house, Sue's words about the importance of spending time together reverberated in her head. She thought, "Well, we didn't plan it, but come Saturday evening, Sue's prescription for us is about to happen."

CHAPTER 25

Rapprochement

As soon as Rocky heard the car honk, he tore down the stairs, overnight bag and baseball glove in hand. "Bye Mom, bye Dad," he shouted as he ran out the screen door. Donna followed him to the car and greeted Matt Sanchez's mother Alicia, who had rolled her window down and greeted Donna with a wide smile.

"Hi, Donna."

"Hi, Alicia," replied Donna, waving a hello and walking up to Alicia's car window. With her hands on the car door, she said, "I appreciate your taking in Rocky. What time should we pick him up tomorrow?"

Alicia answered, "You know we love having Rocky over—it's no trouble at all. Anytime in the morning after ten will be fine."

"Perfect. I'll be there. Rocky, have a great time,

and don't mess up the Sanchez's house."

"I won't Mom. See ya."

Alicia backed out of the driveway, and soon they were gone. "Now," Donna thought, "there's nobody here but us married people."

Bob greeted her at the door. "Alone at last," he said. "How about the living room?"

"Fine," Donna responded.

After they were seated in the living room Bob began. "I'm assuming now is a good time for us to talk about the state of the union."

Donna nodded. "As good as it will ever be."

"Good. I've been waiting a long time to have this conversation. Probably too long, but I was tippy-toeing around, hoping my being nice and agreeable would be enough. Obviously it wasn't since not much has changed."

Donna answered quickly, "Look, I told you it would take time. I don't know what kind of miracle you were expecting."

Bob was expecting a response from Donna, even a sarcastic barb. He continued, "You think I haven't been patient enough." Perhaps this was the time to tell her the truth with compassion, he thought, recalling HEART secret Number Five. So, he plunged in. "I feel unfairly blamed for all our problems, almost like, if San Antonio hadn't happened, everything would be hunky-dory between us, but that's not true, and I think you know it. I now understand why that event upset you so much. I've accepted responsibility and apologized, and we've got other stuff to deal with."

Bob took a breath and looked at her. To his surprise, there was no comeback. She wasn't rebutting him on this point. She sat there calmly. Bob took her silence for agreement and continued.

"From my point of view, our marriage wasn't working long before San Antonio. We were living together and doing a good job as Rocky's parents, but that's about it. But, where was the affection we used to enjoy together—the kindness, the fun, the joking around, the little love pats, the playfulness, the loving looks, the little surprises? It seems like all these signs of love between us had dwindled down to nothing. And like a barometer dropping, our lovemaking disappeared along with everything else."

Donna's face reddened. "You're blaming me for all that? San Antonio aside, I thought you were having an affair with someone in the library, you spend so much time there."

"Yeah, right, I'm getting it on with the dead Hungarians. They're really hot." Donna smiled in spite of herself. "No, I'm not blaming you. We've created this situation together. You and I are great with logistics, but not so great any more with warmth and caring. It's become like an emotional desert around here, and I am dying of thirst. Maybe you are too—I don't know."

"Of course I am. But I'm still here. I'm not looking around." Bob visibly winced at the reference.

"Donna, putting it all on San Antonio makes it all my fault, and that's not fair. I'm feeling blamed and I feel like an exile in my own home. I'm very upset about that."

Bob paused. He was doing his best to respond to the fifth unspoken request: TELL ME THE TRUTH WITH COMPASSION, and realized he was doing a better job with the "truth" part than with the "compassion" part. Since Donna uncharacteristically remained silent, he continued. "I'm not ready to give up on us. I still love you. I love what we had and want to get it back. I'm willing to work together to figure it out. I still think you're a wonderful person, a beautiful, sexy woman, a fantastic mother, a smart, talented businesswoman, and you were a great wife. I want my great wife back, but I don't know how to get there from here."

Donna got up and began pacing back and forth across the living room. Bob sat in silence, waiting anxiously for her response to burst forth. It was her turn.

Finally, Donna began. "There's so much I want to respond to, I hardly know where to begin. First, I'm willing to admit that my own insecurities probably contributed to making your San Antonio behavior maybe a bigger deal than it was. I still don't like it, but hey, you kept your fly zipped—thank you for that!—you apologized, and I do believe you're sincere about not doing it again. I will get over it."

She paused as she walked by one of the end tables where there was a photograph of their wedding, just the two of them gloriously in love. She turned around and looked at him.

"On the other stuff, I don't know. I'm doing my best. I don't think you understand. First, your mother offers me a job. Was it smart to go to work for my mother-in-law? I don't know. But I did it. Then, after I do well selling homes, she offers to sell me half her business at a ridiculously low price with her financing the purchase at a low rate of interest and with the agreement that I take over running the business. You and I discussed the offer at the time. Remember? You said it was an easy decision, far too genereous an offer to refuse. I agreed.

We talked about how it would help pay for Rocky's college education. So, I accept the deal, only now I've got the responsibility of making it work. If the business goes down the tubes, I've got no livelihood and we've got a mountain of debt. So, I'm doing everything I can to make Hartwell Realty a success, and so far it is, but I know the real estate bubble could burst at any time or interest rates could go up or the competition could out-hustle us, and it could all go away. And Molly is counting on me. So, you better believe I'm working flat out all the time. I'm afraid to relax, afraid to let up, afraid to delegate major responsibilites, afraid to let the other realtors handle big customers. The stakes are too big—I can't let it fail."

Donna delivered this doing laps around the living room. Bob was fascinated both by watching her determined movement and by getting a picture of how his wife's mind worked. All of a sudden he remembered it might be a good time to respond to Donna's unspoken request, HEAR AND UNDERSTAND ME.

"So you feel under the gun to make Hartwell Realty successful and that requires maximum effort all the time?"

Donna nodded. "It does. And frankly, your situation is not very different. You're on the final lap of the tenure track, and I don't see you lolly-gagging either. How many cables between the State Department and the U.S. Embassy in Budapest are you going to have to read? I'm surprised your brain hasn't turned to mush already. Maybe the Hungarians weren't promised anything. Maybe they're just a bunch of whiners. What would that mean for your article? Or for your tenure decision? Anyway, I'd put your time in the library against my time showing houses. And I'm not being critical. You have to do what you have to do. I understand. But so do I, for now. These crunches won't last forever. You'll get your tenure. Hartwell Realty will eventually get big enough for me to hire an office manager or establish branch offices, and I'll be able to ease off some. But, as I see it, right now, we're both stuck with our work commitments. I'm sorry it's hard for you—it's hard for me too, but why can't we just tough it out for a few years until both our careers are established? I love you too, and want to stay married, but you won't be fun to be around if you blow tenure, and I won't be fun to be around if I have to explain to Molly why Hartwell Realty went belly up."

Bob was listening hard, dying to interrupt her with responses and rebuttals, thinking to himself, "Hell, you're not much fun to be around right now." But he held to the discipline.

"You think we're both stuck with our work priorities, that there's no relief in sight for the fore-seeable future. And you want me to just pull up my socks and put up with it until both our careers reach the next plateau."

Donna nodded, as if to say this was the only possible plan she could see.

Bob was shaking his head. "I don't know Donna, I appreciate that your loving intention is to keep your commitment to Molly and create economic security for our family, but the cost might be too high. One definition of insanity is doing what you've always done and expecting a different result. I don't get how we're going to make our marriage better if we aren't willing to make any changes. I don't know the answers, but I'm worried about a plan where the main strategy is keeping the status quo and just trying harder."

Donna stopped pacing and came over and sat down on the sofa next to Bob. "I don't have the answers, either, Bob. I wish I did. But I know one change we can make. What would you say to moving out of the guest room and coming back into the bedroom with me?"

Bob gave Donna an impulsive hug. "What would I say? I'd say I'm going to do it right now before you change your mind."

He got up and practically dashed toward the guestroom. "Yippee!" he shouted and did a little dance across the carpet, as Donna shook her head and laughed at her silly husband.

She realized it was the first time she had truly laughed in weeks.

CHAPTER 26

Sunday Morning

Bob woke up the next morning with a big grin on his face. He was back in his own bed again. He had slept next to Donna all night long. His entire body had a warm glow. He reached over for her, but she wasn't there, and then he heard the water running in the shower.

Bob lay there enjoying the languor of a morning in bed. "My own bed." He relished the very sound of the words as he said them. He didn't know whether it was the same for women, but for him the act of making love, in addition to being wonderful on its own, left him feeling loved in a way that nothing else could. So, after three weeks of domestic cold war and frigid relations, it felt especially good to be back on intimate terms with his lovely wife.

Marvin had once told him that for him "after

a fight, love was the best," hinting that he may even have picked fights with Sue just to savor the sweet reconciliation afterwards. Bob would never do that. Aside from being too manipulative, it might cost him another three weeks of forced abstinence. Who needed that?

Lying there and listening to the sounds of the shower, Bob did a quick HEART Check of yesterday's conversation with Donna about the state of their union. He knew he had done well with the unspoken requests, HEAR AND UNDERSTAND ME and TELL ME THE TRUTH WITH COMPASSION, but he realized on reflection that he had also honored the other three. With the request, EVEN IF YOU DISAGREE, PLEASE DON'T MAKE ME WRONG, he had expressed reservations about the status quo of their work commitments but had done so in a respectful, non-blaming way. On ACKNOWLEDGE THE GREATNESS WITHIN ME, he had told Donna how much he loved and valued her in all her various roles. And on REMEMBER TO LOOK FOR MY LOVING INTENTIONS, he had even done that in regard to her dedication to making Hartwell Realty a success. "Damn," he thought, "I hit all five in one conversation. I'm getting good at this."

As Bob reflected more deeply on that conversation, he wondered whether there might not be some relationship between honoring all five of Donna's unspoken requests and being invited to move back into their shared bedroom. Bob was still lying in bed when his mind switched tracks and went over to his second favorite topic, the Hungarian Revolution of 1956. He was trying to recall something Donna had said the night before—what was it?—oh yeah, that maybe the Hungarians were just a bunch of whiners. Dwelling for a moment on that amusing comment, all of a sudden he had a flash of insight, the kind that seems so obvious after you've had it: the reason he wasn't finding a "smoking gun" offer to the Hungarians in the diplomatic cables was. . . . .THAT IT DIDN'T EXIST!! No American official had promised American military support. The Hungarians had received constant encouragement from Radio Free Europe and, knowing that it was part of our foreign policy operation, had, with more than a dollop of wishful thinking, inferred that the U.S. would come to the aid of a rebellion against the Soviet authority. He would take a look at communications between the State Department and the semi-autonomous Radio Free Europe, but he knew he would find no incriminating evidence.

This insight produced a mixed reaction. The bad news was that his article would not make a big splash. It would not revise the accepted version of Cold War history. The good news was he now had his article. It would not be spectacular, but it would be solid. Was that enough for him to ice tenure? He didn't know.

Meanwhile, Donna, enjoying a long, hot shower, felt relieved that the tension of the San Antonio event and the subsequent in-house separation had been resolved. She loved Bob and saw him as a good man and devoted husband and father, but in her mind there was still a cloud hanging over them, the dilemma of how to sustain and build their marriage in the face of their implacable career imperatives.

She decided for the moment just to enjoy the warmth of the shower and of the sweetness of their reconciliation and put off the dilemma for another day.

CHAPTER 27

Generations

As she drove down the boulevard toward the Hartwell Realty office, Molly was thinking about Donna and Bob and their shaky marriage, and what she could do to help. Molly felt she had a great relationship with Donna, one that was able to embrace both a smooth, harmonious business partnership and a loving, supportive mother-in-law/daughter-in-law friendship. She admired Donna tremendously, her fantastic energy, her ability to create instant rapport with clients, and her demanding yet compassionate leadership of the Hartwell Realty staff. Plus her parenting of Rocky. Bob had often said—although, come to think of it, not lately—how lucky he felt to be married to Donna. Molly agreed wholeheartedly.

Nevertheless, there remained an unmarked boundary surrounding Bob and Donna's marriage that

Molly recognized and had never crossed. To be able to work well together, it was tacitly understood that the bumpy road of the marital relationship was not to be broached by either of them.

This posed a dilemma for Molly. She wasn't even sure what she wanted to say. But if divorce was even a remote possibility, she didn't want to be a bystander. Even if her intervention might injure her relationship with Donna, with the high stakes of Rocky's well being, Molly would take the risk. Since she didn't really know where Donna's head was, she decided that some data collection and diagnosis would be in order prior to any advice or coaching. As she entered the Hartwell Realty parking area, she could see Donna in her office through the glass window. Talking to Donna was definitely her first order of business.

After greeting the few staff members present, Molly knocked on Donna's open door. Donna was on the phone but motioned Molly to come in. Molly took a seat in a comfortable chair across the desk from Donna, who ended the phone call and came around to greet and kiss Molly. Donna sat down in another comfortable chair next to Molly.

"Hey, Molly, what are you up to?"

"Nothing much. Harry and I finished delivering our Meals on Wheels, and he went home to tend the roses. So, I decided to come over and check in with my favorite daughter-in-law."

Donna laughed. "Easy to be the favorite when you're the only. How are you doing?"

Molly got up, closed the door, and gathered herself. "Well, I'm mostly good, but my grapevine husband told me you and Bob were on the outs, and that has been worrying me."

Donna reached over and put her hand on top of Molly's. "Oh dear, I'm sorry. I can imagine how upsetting that would be for you."

When Molly nodded, Donna went on. "I think I can reassure you and allay your fear. Bob and I are not in the process of getting a divorce. We're working on some issues. Neither of us is feeling real happy about the way things are going right now."

Molly was indeed relieved that they weren't on the brink of divorce. She decided to go one step further. "Do you feel like talking about what the things are that you're referring to?"

"Sure. We're living the parallel lives of two workaholics who take turns parenting their son and who never have any time to be together, and both of us have great reasons to do exactly what we're doing. It makes for two great careers and one lousy marriage."

Molly was shocked to hear Donna's situation described so baldly. Not that she couldn't have figured it out; just that she had never even thought about it. Molly had never pictured Donna as a workaholic. "I know about Bob's situation with tenure and all. But tell me why you think you have to be a workaholic to run Hartwell Realty."

"Well, Molly, I'll tell you, but I think it's about things you already know."

"Really?" said Molly in all honesty.

"I know how hard you worked to build this business and now you've entrusted it to me. You depend on it for income and for a part of your retirement. And you're counting on me to pay off the loan you so generously made so I could buy in. If I mess up, you're the one who gets hurt the most, and I will never, ever let that happen. So I am doing whatever it takes, and what it takes is most week-day evenings and most weekends showing houses, particularly the high-end houses that I have a better track record selling than the other staff. Bob resents that I'm not around more, but he's off in the library reading about a bunch of crazy Hungarians, so he's strung out too."

Molly listened with growing concern. She rubbed her hands together, as if it would help her ponder this issue more clearly. Had she inadvertently put this pressure on Donna? Had she said something to make Donna treat Hartwell Realty like a life-or-death issue? She searched her mind but came up empty. She looked warmly at Donna and asked quietly, "Dear, you're working like a madwoman out of concern for me?" Molly shook her head incredulously, mouth agape. "You think this is something I want you to be doing?"

Donna slowly nodded her head.

"Now, Donna, you listen," she said, turning to face her daughter-in-law and speaking with great intensity. "This is the horse's mouth speaking. I do not, repeat, DO NOT want you to be a workaholic, to work such long hours that it wounds your marriage. I never did that when I was running the business. Why would you imagine that I'd actually want you to put your marriage at risk? I'm just dumbfounded that you would think that. And I mean, even if it meant Hartwell Realty were to go kaflooey—bankrupt. I love Hartwell Realty, but your marriage and family are far more important to me. If I had to sacrifice one of the two, it would be—what's that expression of Rocky's—oh yes, a slam-dunk. It would be a slam-dunk!" Molly said, proud of using a bit of current slang.

Donna was touched by Molly's support and amused to hear Rocky's expression come from his grandmother. "Molly, I appreciate what you're saying. I know you care more about us as a family than the business, but I feel stuck. I'm trying to make everything work, and I thought I could, but maybe I can't."

"There," thought Donna, "everything is now right out on the table." And she relaxed a bit.

Molly sat back in her chair, straightened her jacket, turned again to Donna and, almost offhandedly, asked, "Can I offer you a little coaching on management?"

"Sure, coach away."

"Your job as manager is to hire people with the talent and skills to be successful realtors. On top of that, you train them, let them go along with you and watch how you are with clients, then you watch how they are with clients and give them feedback, then they show houses to clients on their own. And you review how they do, what they did right on their successes, what they did wrong on lost sales, what they could do better next time. That's your job."

Donna nodded in agreement.

"And then it's their job to show houses on evenings and weekends. Not yours."

Donna was frowning and shaking her head. "Molly, if I do what you're proposing, it's going to cost us sales, particularly on the high end properties that I currently handle. We have good people, but they are going to make mistakes, expensive mistakes."

"If they make mistakes, you help them get corrected for the next time. But you don't have to do your job and their jobs. You just do yours."

"And . . . ?" Donna asked.

"And, because you're the owner and manager," continued Molly with great authority, "you get to spend evenings and weekends with your family, with your husband and son, who have been bereft of your wonderful presence and missing the hell out of it."

Donna laughed out loud as her last resistance dissolved. It was a laugh of relief and a laugh of delight at having such a strong and loving mother-in-law.

"So, that's my coaching" said Molly, laughing, too. And, waving her hand in the air, she added, "Stop doing everybody's job. It's too much. Too much for you and far too much for your family. And stop using my alleged expectations as your excuse for being a workaholic. It's bogus. I have no such expectations, believe me."

Donna was listening with her mouth hanging open. She had never heard Molly talk like this, with such clarity and conviction. And she knew Molly was 100% right. She had been afraid to trust that the staff could learn and grow to be as effective at sales as she was. And she had made assumptions about what Molly expected without ever asking. What really felt freeing was Molly's willingness to share the risk of Hartwell Realty failing rather than risk their family breaking apart. "What a mother-in-law I have!" she thought. Then she decided to share it.

"Molly, let me tell you, you are one gem of a mother-in-law. They don't make 'em like you any more. Thanks for giving me permission not to be obsessive about the business, and for giving me some ideas on how I can gradually ease off and be home more. That's all I can say. Thanks."

As Molly stood up to leave, Donna leaned over, gave the older woman a hug, and began to cry. "Thank you so much," she sobbed.

Molly held her and thought, "This is a good day for the Hartwell family. All three generations."

CHAPTER 28

Tennis

The next day, when Bob returned from the university, he was surprised to see his father's black Chrysler 300 in the driveway. As he walked through the house, he heard familiar voices outside and followed them to the back yard. There he beheld a remarkable sight. His 68-year-old father, wearing Bob's catcher's mitt, was engaged in a spirited warm up with Rocky, who was throwing a hard ball from a full wind-up. Harry was also doubling as umpire, declaring each pitch to be either a strike or a ball.

"Ball three, outside," Harry announced.

"Grandpa, could you crouch down and give me a better target?" Rocky implored.

"Sorry, Rocky, the old knees don't bend that way any more. Chuck it in here, big fella', right here!" Harry made an effort to put his glove right in the center of where home plate might be.

"Strike one! All right!"

As Rocky saw his father, he stopped throwing and greeted him. "Hi Dad, I got me a new catcher."

"So I see."

Harry said, "Hi, Bob. I don't think the substitution is permanent. This is hard work."

Bob smiled. "Did you volunteer or were you drafted?"

"I drafted him." It was Donna's voice. She emerged from the house dressed in her tennis whites. "C'mon, Bob," she said enthusiastically, "get in the house and put on your tennis stuff. You have a tennis date."

"Donna, I haven't picked up a tennis racquet in over two years."

"Right. We're going to end that streak today. Get your stuff on. I'll wait out here. I want to watch your dad fire it back to our pitcher."

Bob went off, as directed, to change. As he pulled open dresser drawers looking for his long neglected tennis shorts, his mind was buzzing. "I guess this means Donna doesn't have any appointments tonight. Great."

A few minutes later, while tying the laces of his tennis shoes, he mused, "Boy, Dad's arm is going to be sore as hell tomorrow, but what a treat for Rocky to pitch to his grandfather."

By the time Bob came downstairs, Donna had their tennis racquets, a can of balls, water bottles and towels out and ready to go.

"Hop in," she said.

Once in the car, a teasing and grinning Bob asked her, "Are we going to do this once every two years, or what? What's happening here?"

Donna was driving. "I had a great talk with Molly today. She helped me see how I can do my job without being an absentee wife. So, I thought we'd inaugurate the new era with a unique event, just to see how you like it. And," she added with emphasis, "if you like it, we can do it more, maybe even play mixed doubles, if you get good enough."

Bob laughed. It was an old familiar, relaxed laugh she had not heard in a while. She knew he was competitive enough to appreciate the challenge. "Well, I used to be a decent player. Maybe after the rust wears off, I can get there, if I really work at it," Bob said with a slight sarcastic edge.

"Seriously," Donna added. "I want to talk about how we can rearrange our lives and have more time together. It doesn't have to be tennis."

"Tennis is great, but tell me what happened today," Bob replied.

"Molly sort of set me straight on a few things," she said. "She suggested that I work on becoming more of a coach and trainer and less of a doer, which would free up a lot of evenings and weekends. I haven't figured out how to implement it yet or how it's all going to work, but that's where I'm headed. With Molly's full support," she added.

"Amazing!" he said. "Wonders will never cease. First I see my big old dad wearing a catcher's mitt. Then my obsessive, workaholic wife gathers me up for a tennis game. This is quite a strange day."

"That's what we need, dear. Lots and lots of strange, wonderful days. Get used to it. This is only the first."

"I could get used to it," he said, putting his hand

on her knee. Then, he leaned over and whispered in her ear, "I'm almost through with the Hungarians."

She laughed. "This is truly an amazing day."

"Summer is almost upon us," he observed, still whispering in her ear. "I could get very used to this."

CHAPTER 29

Brainstorm

Bob and Donna came into the kitchen exhausted but happy from their vigorous tennis match.

Bob said, "I guess the drinks are on me since I got my butt kicked." He took two ice-cold beers from the refrigerator and handed one to Donna.

"Thanks, Hartwell," she said, lifting the bottle in the air, as if toasting him. She added, with teasing humor, "You did good for your first outing in two years. You have real promise."

As they sat down, Donna saw a note on the breakfast table. She leaned over, peered at it, and read it out loud. "Went out for a pizza. Be back around 7:30. Dad."

She turned to Bob. "I guess Harry survived his stint behind the plate."

They sat quietly and both drank their beers

right from the bottles. They both realized they had not spent a fun evening like this in, what was it, almost two years. The feeling of mutual delight felt almost foreign to them, but it was also too beautiful and powerful to mar.

When they looked up at each other, Bob said, "Boy, nothing like a cold beer on a hot day. You know, tennis is fun. I forgot how much I liked it."

Donna put her beer down on the counter and said, "I have a feeling a lot of things could be fun again, if we ever found time to do them together."

Bob said, "I have an idea. Let's brainstorm a list, a sort of wish list, of things we might like to do together. Then we can go through the list and see which ones we actually want to follow through on."

"Sounds good," said Donna, moving toward the telephone nook. "Here's some paper. I've got the pen."

"Let's do it," said Bob.

"Okay," Donna hesitated, remembering Bob's love of debate, "but in a brainstorm, anything goes, right?" She wanted their ground rules to be perfectly clear. "No judgements, no groans, no faces, no vetoes. These are just ideas or possibilities." She waited, pen poised.

"Okay by me," agreed Bob readily. "So, put down 'a weekly tennis match.'"

"I'm adding some mixed doubles matches, okay?"

"Great," he replied. "How about cultural events like movies or plays?"

"Or concerts?" she asked, writing.

"Or, heaven help us, lectures at the College?" suggested Bob with a twinkle in his eye.

Donna didn't write that one down. She looked

up at him. "I wouldn't go that far."

"Ah, ah, ah," said Bob wagging his finger at her. "Are we making a judgement?"

"Oh, right." She bent over and scribbled "lectures" on her note pad. Then, more brightly, she asked, "How about bicycle rides?"

"This assumes I have a bicycle."

"Ah, ah, ah," she looked up smiling. "No logistics."

"Okay, bicycles. Then add hiking."

Donna put her pen down and said, "Sue told me she and Marvin have a weekly untouchable date night. How about us having a date night?"

"You mean, all to ourselves? No Rocky?"

"No Rocky. Just us, you and me alone."

"To do what?"

"To do anything we want." She turned to Bob. He looked puzzled. "It could change from week to week."

He turned his head and smiled, as it dawned on him what Donna was suggesting. "Damn, a weekly date night." He paused. "Is it Wednesday for them? Marvin and Sue I mean?"

"Yes," she said, surprised. "Why do you ask?"

"I can never get Marvin to do anything on Wednesday nights. He always says he has a prior commitment. That son of a gun."

"So," she asked, "does a date night for us sound like a good idea?"

"Fantastic! Write it down. And I'll even go you one further. How about a whole weekend away, with Mom and Dad looking after Rocky?" He felt outrageously free doing this brainstorming. Even if nothing came of it, he thought, it is really fun just to think of being alone together.

"Sure," said Donna. "We can even do a vacation together."

"You mean just the two of us? What about Rocky?"

"Oh, I forgot to tell you," she said with a smirk. "He wants to go to baseball camp this summer for two weeks."

"Hot dog!" said Bob. "This brainstorm list is really hopping!"

"I want to make another request," she added, "that we have dinners together as a family."

"Put it on the list," said Bob. "And maybe now we can take weekend excursions with Rocky, like to Washington or Gettysburg."

The always-well-organized Donna inserted a question. "Are we done with items just for the two of us? We seem to have drifted over to items that would include our little Rock person."

"I've got one last item for just the two of us," said Bob with a shy look, "that we take an occasional shower together."

"That's a great one to end on," agreed Donna. She held up the note pad for Bob to see the long list they had made. "Now, my good man, how are we going to decide which ones to actually do?" She paused. "We are going to do some of them, aren't we?"

Lifting his beer, he said with a swagger in his voice, "I think we should do all of them." After a moment, he added, "But, maybe not all at once."

"You mean, keep the list and just start doing some of the easier ones?"

"Yeah," he said. "We don't have to be too organized about it. It can be sort of organic, a mixture of planned and spontaneous."

"Okay," said Donna, realizing that Bob preferred the spontaneous, while she preferred the planned. "But, how about we sit down once a week and go over what we did and what we want to do the next week, so it doesn't get away from us."

"A wonderful idea," said Bob, getting up from his side of the table and coming around to give Donna a kiss. In an afterthought, he added, "It's so great to have a wife with these managerial skills."

Donna accepted the kiss and the compliment graciously. "Thank you, dear. And it's great to have a husband who appreciates them."

Having completed their brainstorming list, Bob and Donna went upstairs to shower and, incidentally, to implement the final item on their together list.

CHAPTER 30

Celebration

June 8th was Bob and Donna's 14th anniversary, and they had made a conscious decision about how they wanted to celebrate. They invited Bob's parents, Harry and Molly, and they invited their best friends, Sue and Marvin Rogers, along with their children Carol and Annette to a lavish barbecue at their home. After dinner, Rocky invited the girls to join him in playing some computer games, and they followed him inside.

Now, in the quiet evening, when the dishes had been cleared and everyone around the picnic table seemed relaxed and happy, Bob brought out six champagne glasses and two ice-cold bottles of Dom Perignon. He opened the first bottle with a loud pop and carefully poured a small amount into each of the glasses.

When the glasses were passed out, he raised his own glass and said, "I have a few toasts I would like to make. First and foremost to you, Donna, my bride of fourteen years: For putting up with my frailties, for forgiving my transgressions, and for continuing to be devoted and loving beyond reason."

Everybody drank up to a chorus of "Hear, hear!"

Bob called for all the glasses to be put together on the table again, and he poured a bit more champagne into each. Again, he asked them to lift their glasses for another toast. Bob continued. "Next, to you, our dear friends Sue and Marvin. Hillary Clinton once said, 'It takes a village to raise a child.' Well, apparently, it takes very good friends to support a marriage, particularly one undergoing some wobbly moments."

They all chuckled.

Bob went on. "To you, Sue, for helping Donna see the importance of our spending time together no matter what else is going on and providing a model of that. And to you, Marvin, for educating me about the power of gestures and for teaching me that sending flowers to an angry wife is a profound and rewarding act of faith."

This line drew laughs, especially from Sue, and once again, to a hearty "Hear, hear!" the glasses were drained.

Bob called for a third re-enactment of the traditional ritual, but discovered he needed to open a second bottle to re-fill all the glasses a third time.

"Last but not least," Bob began with unaccustomed seriousness, "I want to acknowledge my extraordinary parents. Mom, if there were an Academy Award or a Vince Lombardi trophy for Best Mother-in-law, you would win it hands down for somehow cracking the case that Donna had around being a workaholic. I don't quite understand how you did it, but thank you and God bless you. By the way, I am happy to report that my own bout of workaholism of the Hungarian variety is also about to end. And Dad, I can honestly say that the gift you gave me of the five HEART secrets literally saved our marriage. Before our conversation on the porch, I was doing everything wrong. I was hunkering down, defending myself, becoming impatient, feeling sorry for myself, not trying to understand Donna's point of view. I was digging myself and our marriage into a deeper and deeper hole. Learning about the five unspoken requests and beginning to honor them made all the difference. I believe that information you gave me allowed me to turn things around. So, from the bottom of my heart, thank you, Dad, for your wisdom and for your courage in sharing it with your wayward son."

Another round of "Hear, hear!" and the glasses were emptied again. This time Molly called for her turn. The six glasses were returned to the center of the table, Molly took the bottle and poured. "Just a very little sip for each this time, as I'm afraid we'll soon be drunk."

The others agreed. Then, she stood up and held her glass high.

Everyone grew quiet. Even the evening sky was still.

She began, "Well, I agree. We were all a pretty darn good support system. But now I want to toast you, Bob and Donna, the couple whose fourteenth anniversary we are celebrating. All the help in the world would have come to naught if you two hadn't been committed to your marriage and to remaining a family. By being willing to listen to advice, to work on your marriage, and to change your established way of life, you have kept something precious alive."

The group were all holding their glasses and murmuring "Hear, hear!" but Molly hushed them. "I'm not finished yet."

The group fell silent.

"And not only for yourselves," Molly began. "The greatest beneficiary of your commitment is Rocky, because now he gets to keep having both loving parents in his life and in his home every day. What a gift that is and what a blessing. Rocky can handle the Mets losing. He can even handle the Rottweilers losing. As long as he has his family. So, here's my toast to you, Bob and Donna, for having the love and perseverance to do whatever it took to keep your family together."

More clinking of glasses and even more enthusiastic shouts of "Hear, hear!"

Donna stood up. "I'm going to get the last word here, since we're running out of champagne."

Donna measured out the remaining contents of the bottle into each of the glasses, passed them around, and began.

"Thank you all for being there for us in the crunch, and, especially thank you, Bob, for hanging in with me even when I was gone a lot. Maybe worka-holism is the real infidelity. Anyway, I love you. I feel lucky and blessed to be your wife these fourteen years, and I may even learn to like baseball."

Everyone broke up with laughter at that, and clinked glasses for their final round of champagne.

CHAPTER 31

Valedictory

It was the usual buzz of conversation among the participants before the weekly meeting of Unfaithful Anonymous got under way. Bob had been talking quietly to the group leader.

When the time came to start the meeting, the leader invited everyone to get a cup of coffee, if they wished, and be seated. Then, he said, "Bob has asked to be the first to speak tonight. So, if you would all give him your full attention, we'll begin."

All eyes turned to Bob, curious to hear what he had to say.

"My name is Bob," he began, using the traditional introduction of all Anonymous groups, "and, contrary to my earlier evasions, I WAS an unfaithful husband. I am here, I earnestly hope, for the last time. I have come to say goodbye and to thank you for your help in penetrating my smug defenses and heightening my awareness of the true meaning of fidelity."

Bob looked around at the group and thought he detected in their eyes a look of "Thank goodness, he got it!" He would reassure them that he had.

"I have learned that being faithful to a marriage means more than merely not being unfaithful, although that is surely one component. I now understand that being faithful means making my marriage my primary commitment and not allowing that commitment to be eclipsed or slighted by anything, regardless of reasons or temptations."

There were nods of agreement all around the circle.

"I have thought about how I might adequately acknowledge you for your support," Bob went on, "and I have decided to leave you all with a gift that is small in size but perhaps not in impact. It's a gift that I received from someone else, but you here tonight are the ones who put me in the starting gate. You helped me to know what to look for in finding my way.

"Last month's Feedback session helped me, in your words, 'to buy the saddle' of my infidelity. That provided the opening, the starting point to re-build my marriage, but it was only the starting point. More was required. What I still needed I received from a most unlikely source—my father. The gift he gave me is the gift that I am going to pass on to you, to use, if you wish, to re-build your own marriages. It is a simple but profound insight into human relationships.

"My father told me that there are five unspoken requests that everyone, and especially our spouses, are making of us all the time, and that if we honor these five unspoken requests, our wives will feel respected and loved."

The group's interest was clearly growing, Bob could tell by their faces, but they remained silent, as was the rule in Unfaithful Anonymous when someone else was speaking. So, Bob continued.

"Don't ask me how my dad figured out this set of requests, or how or why they work, but I tried it and it worked for me beyond all expectations or hope." With utter confidence he added, "Against all odds, my family is back together.

"So, what are these five unspoken requests, you ask? Ah, that is my gift to you. I have had these requests printed up on handy little cards that you can carry around with you. I have a card for each of you, and 100 extras for future participants of this Unfaithful Anonymous chapter.

"The five requests can be a little hard to remember. For that reason, they conform to the acronym HEART. My parting gift to you, then, is the FIVE SECRETS OF MARRIAGE FROM THE HEART, truly a symbol of my heartfelt thanks to you."

THE *5* SECRETS
OF MARRIAGE FROM THE HEART

Hear and understand me.

Even if you disagree, please don't make me wrong.

Acknowledge the greatness within me.

Remember to look for my loving intentions.

Tell me the truth with compassion.

ABOUT THE AUTHORS

Jack Rosenblum, Ed.D., J.D., and Corinne Dugas, M.Ed., have been married since 1977 and have a daughter in college. Working with couples is one of the things they most enjoy doing together. They co-created the workshop "LoveWorks: Skills for the journey of committed partnership," teach the Five Secrets, and practice what they preach.

Jack has over 30 years experience as a management consultant helping top teams learn to work together in harmony. Prior to that he was one of the first Peace Corps Volunteers and chief of New York City's drug prevention program for youth. He has a special gift for helping people acknowledge and work through conflict all the way to the end and come out the other side as allies and friends. He does this with married couples as well as with work teams. Jack is the author of numerous articles and co-author of *Managing From the Heart*. His sessions are noted for a rare combination of clarity, empathy, and gentle humor.

Corinne is a lifelong educator. After receiving her Master's degree in counseling, she was a facilitator conducting training-for-trainers and personal growth workshops for non-profit organizations. Before that, she directed an adult education center and taught junior high social studies in the inner city of Baltimore. Currently, in addition to her couples work, she is a Creative Memories consultant helping individuals create photo heritage legacies. Clients and workshop participants appreciate the warmth, compassion, insight, and generosity of spirit Corinne brings to her counseling and teaching.

Jack and Corinne live in Deerfield, Massachusetts. Both of them are competitive tennis players, bicyclists, avid readers and movie goers, and serious Boston Red Sox fans.

THE *5* SECRETS
OF MARRIAGE FROM THE HEART

Hear and understand me.

Even if you disagree, please don't make me wrong.

Acknowledge the greatness within me.

Remember to look for my loving intentions.

Tell me the truth with compassion.

THE *5* SECRETS
OF MARRIAGE FROM THE HEART

Hear and understand me.

Even if you disagree, please don't make me wrong.

Acknowledge the greatness within me.

Remember to look for my loving intentions.

Tell me the truth with compassion.

THE *5* SECRETS
OF MARRIAGE FROM THE HEART

Hear and understand me.

Even if you disagree, please don't make me wrong.

Acknowledge the greatness within me.

Remember to look for my loving intentions.

Tell me the truth with compassion.

THE *5* SECRETS
OF MARRIAGE FROM THE HEART

Hear and understand me.

Even if you disagree, please don't make me wrong.

Acknowledge the greatness within me.

Remember to look for my loving intentions.

Tell me the truth with compassion.

Thank you for selecting a book from
TATE PUBLISHING

Tate Publishing is committed to excellence in the publishing industry. Our staff of highly trained professionals—editors, creative designers, graphic artists, and marketing personnel—work together to produce the very finest book products available. The company reflects in every aspect the philosophy established by the founders based on Psalms 68:11, "The Lord gave the word and great was the company of those who published it."

If you would like further information, please call 1-888-361-9473 or visit our website at www.tatepublishing.com.

TATE PUBLISHING LLC
127 E. Trade Center Terrace
Mustang, Oklahoma 73064 USA